ADVANCE PRAISE

"I encourage anyone to get ahold of this book. Whether you're a woman, or a man, who has a daughter or a wife who wants to be more empowered or stand up more for herself, this is a great book. It's great for yourself and for a gift. If you want to be a gutsier person by standing up for yourself and allowing yourself to understand and use your own power, this is the book that will help get you there."

—**Jack Canfield,** author of the Chicken Soup for the Soul Series and *The Success Principles*

"If we're lucky, one day we wake up and realize that there's more to life than climbing the ladder of success and piling up wealth. That's the moment we glimpse possibilities that previously seemed impossible. *Gutsy Women Win* is your bridge to this new future, where you discover the contributions you were born to make on planet Earth, as well as a guide to how to make those possibilities a reality. Read it. Learn it. Do it!"

—**Kimberly Wiefling,** author of *Scrappy Project Management*, global business consultant, and gutsy Silicon Valley woman

"Many times, when you think of a "gutsy" person, you think of the flamboyant daredevil who hogs the spotlight. In *Gutsy Women Win*, Pat Obuchowski shows you that nothing could be further from the truth. Pat reveals that "gutsy" is YOU. *Gutsy Women Win* gives you the blueprint for living your life with more gusto, passion, and verve and the permission to play the bigger game called *Your Life*."

—**Dana Wilde,** best-selling author of
Train Your Brain and host of *The Mind Aware Show*

"Pat Obuchowski embodies the word gutsy. I have witnessed firsthand that Pat means what she says. Her whole being is so full of energy, enthusiasm, and positivity, you cannot escape the results of her presence, either in person or in her writing."

—**John Kiskaddon,** cofounder, Harper Greer

"Pat Obuchowski shows you how to find the courage you never knew you had to achieve what you never thought you could accomplish. As an author, coach, and client, she has helped me and she can help you too."

—**Steve Harrison,** www.authorsuccess.com

"Pat Obuchowski can help anyone play a bigger game! Regardless of how successful (or not) you feel, *Gutsy Women Win* will inspire you to get gutsy and get going. Warm, thought-provoking, and clear, it is a must read for those who want to change something in themselves or the world! You don't want to miss this book!"

—**Elizabeth Crook,** founder Orchard Advisors;
Think Bigger, Act Smarter, Live Richer

"*Gutsy Women Win* will inspire you to play big, get gutsy, and get going. Author Pat Obuchowski is the ultimate Bigger Game player and encourages us all to stop playing small in life. It's time to get gutsy folks, and Pat shows us the way in this inspiring and must-read book."

—**Rick Tamlyn,** author of *Play Your Bigger Game*
and cofounder of The Bigger Game

"Our world so desperately needs women to own their power and to engage in playing bigger games in a way that is fulfilling and nourishing. Thanks to executive coach and author Pat Obuchowski for this wonderful book! I'm delighted to endorse this engaging tribute to the original 'gusty woman,' Laura Whitworth."

—**Karen Kimsey-House,** cofounder,
The Coaches Training Institute

"*Gutsy Women Win* shows you how you can win at whatever games you consciously decide to play in your life. Pat explains a model that will easily work for you as you step into becoming more powerful, confident, and learn to lead from any seat at the table. This book will challenge you in ways you haven't been challenged before, and, trust me, that is a good thing. It will help you get gutsy and get going."

—**Leslie Grossman,** author of *Link Out: How to Turn Your Network into a Chain of Lasting Connections*

"Pat Obuchowski was a premier success coach for eWomenNetwork and her guidance to women was invaluable. *Gutsy Women Win* is the perfect stimulus for igniting your dreams and passion. This book will move you to action!"

—**Kim Yancey,** cofounder and president eWomenNetwork

"*Gutsy Women Win* is awesome! It is THE book to get if you want to find the courage to ask for and get what you want in both your professional and personal life. I know Pat is a Gutsy Woman and she will help you get gutsy too."

—**Tracy "Twinkie" Byrd,** Award Winning Casting Director and Founder of Twinkie's Hollywood Monologue Slam

GUTSY WOMEN WIN

How to GET GUTSY and GET GOING

PAT OBUCHOWSKI

RIVER GROVE
BOOKS

Published by River Grove Books
Austin, TX
www.rivergrovebooks.com

Courtney Ruby and Sandy Hoffman have changed jobs since they were interviewed for this book, but the author has retained the use of the present tense in their stories.

Distributed by River Grove Books

Design and composition by Greenleaf Book Group and Sheila Parr
Cover design by Greenleaf Book Group and Sheila Parr

For permission to reproduce copyrighted material, grateful acknowledgment is made to the following sources:

Quote by Robert Greenleaf. Copyright © 1970 by Robert Greenleaf. Used by permission of The Greenleaf Center. www.greenleaf.org.

From *A Return to Love: Reflections on the Principles of A Course in Miracles* by Marianne Williamson. Copyright © 1992 by Marianne Williamson. Reproduced by permission of HarperCollins Publishers.

From *The Scottish Himalayan Expedition* by W. H. Murray. Copyright © 1951. Reproduced by permission of Orion Publishing Group Limited.

From Laura Whitworth's blog. Reproduced by permission

Cataloging-in-Publication data is available.

Print ISBN: 978-1-63299-102-7

eBook ISBN: 978-1-63299-103-4

First Edition

This book is dedicated to all the game changers in the world
and to everyone who says no to business as usual.
Know you make a difference.
Know you are valued.
Know you are seen.

Until one is committed
there is a hesitancy,
the chance to draw back,
always ineffectiveness.

Concerning all acts of initiative (and creation),
there is one elementary truth,
the ignorance of which kills countless ideas and splendid plans:
That the moment one definitely commits oneself,
then Providence moves, too.

All sorts of things occur to help one that would
never otherwise have occurred.

A whole stream of events issues from the decision,
raising in one's favor all manner
of unforeseen incidents, meetings and material assistance,
which no man could have dreamt would come his way.
I learned a deep respect for one of Goethe's couplets:
"Whatever you can do or dream you can, begin it.
Boldness has a genius, power and magic in it!"

From *The Scottish Himalayan Expedition* (1951)
By W. H. Murray

CONTENTS

PREFACE A Tribute to Laura Whitworth............................. xiii

INTRODUCTION Are You Ready to Get Gutsy and Get Going? 1

CHAPTER 1 Learning The Bigger Game Model™ Game Board 9

CHAPTER 2 My First (Intentional) Bigger Game 31

CHAPTER 3 Dru Rivers, Co-owner of Full Belly Farms 41

CHAPTER 4 Libby Traubman, Cofounder of the Jewish-Palestinian
Living Room Dialogue Groups 47

CHAPTER 5 Courtney Ruby, Former City Auditor
of Oakland, California.................................... 57

CHAPTER 6 Sandy Hoffman, Former Chief Diversity Officer,
Cisco Systems 67

CHAPTER 7 Anne Firth Murray, Founding President of
the Global Fund for Women............................. 75

CHAPTER 8 Shari Spencer, Mixed Martial Arts Athlete Manager 83

CHAPTER 9 Linda Alepin, Founding Director of the
Global Women's Leadership Network 91

CHAPTER 10 All About The Bigger Game: Investment Piece.......... 97

CHAPTER 11 All About The Bigger Game: Allies Piece............... 109

CHAPTER 12 All About The Bigger Game: Sustainability Piece 121

CHAPTER 13 All About The Bigger Game: Assess Piece 129

CHAPTER 14 Who Are You Becoming? 137

CONCLUSION My Vision for You, Gutsy Woman 145

AN INVITATION TO GET GUTSY AND GET GOING............................147

ACKNOWLEDGMENTS 149

AUTHOR Q & A..151

ABOUT THE AUTHOR 159

Preface

....

A TRIBUTE TO LAURA WHITWORTH

In 2005, several years after I entered the profession of coaching, I received a call I never imagined I would receive. The call was from Laura Whitworth, one of the cofounders of the coaching and certification school I attended, Coaches Training Institute (CTI). She was in the process of creating The Bigger Game Company, which would bring to the world the social and leadership change model she and cofounder Rick Tamlyn developed when they realized that people have a deep yearning to make a difference in this wild, wonderful, and wacky world—they just don't know how. No matter what their clients asked to be coached on, they all went through a pretty common range of elements to move into action around what they wanted to change in their lives. Those elements eventually became The Bigger Game™ model.

Laura was looking for someone to assist her in growing the company and running the Bigger Game training and certification programs. Due to my corporate business background, which was rare in the coaching community, I came strongly recommended as someone who could consult with her on this project.

What I could not believe was that there was a possibility I would be working with Laura Whitworth, one of the most admired leaders in the coaching community. She was a force that impacted thousands of individuals' lives by helping them learn how to be "Game Changers" and allowing and encouraging them to express their own talents and creativity. She did this by challenging and encouraging them to "say no to business as usual."

I scheduled a telephone conversation with Laura to see if we were a match. After a very brief conversation, we both knew we would be working together. She invited me to join her in spreading this work. I became an immediate ally invested in her bigger game.

Looking back at Laura's invitation, I now know I was fully prepared to accept it as I had made two life-changing decisions during the previous few months. The first was to attend The Bigger Game workshop in London, and the second was to immediately follow up with a related workshop in California—this one led by Laura.

One of my strengths is learning. I am always looking at the latest research on human behavior, neuroscience, and new leadership development models that my clients can benefit from. Because the coaching profession was very young at the time, I wanted to experience coaching on an international level. I heard there was a Bigger Game workshop happening in London. I decided this was my opportunity to learn about the model as well as learn about coaching in another country.

Two of CTI's senior workshop leaders and coaches, Rick Tamlyn and L. A. Reding (who was my first coach), led the workshop. For three days, I explored what I was doing in both my professional and my personal life. I felt as if I were on a precipice, looking forward, but hanging on to my past. It was a very scary place to be, as I had to make a conscious decision about who I was becoming. I was no longer letting my future happen by chance. I chose consciously and with intention who I was becoming and would no longer leave my life and next steps to chance.

I saw the same thing happening to those around me. I saw the power of an individual deciding to truly play a bigger game in her or his life. I wanted in. I wanted more. At the time of the London workshop, I still didn't know exactly what my Bigger Game was, but I knew I wanted to live my life with more intention and with more impact.

When I came back home to the San Francisco Bay area, I immediately signed up for an advanced Bigger Game workshop. This is where I met the power named Laura Whitworth. I walked into the room, saw her, and knew why she was so admired, respected, and feared all at the same time. I could feel her strength and power from across the room.

When I walked up to her and introduced myself, I immediately had the feeling I did not want to disappoint her. I wanted her respect and, in some odd but very deep way, I wanted to make this stranger feel proud of me.

When I finished the workshop, I knew what my Bigger Game was, and I knew it would become a reality. Laura had agreed to be an ally in my Bigger Game and I was well on my way.

The game that I was playing was to support women in their bigger work and to help them realize they can and do make a difference: in their family, neighborhood, work, community, city, nation, and even the world. I want to help them wake up to what they, or others, had put to sleep for so long. I want to help them leave the comfort zones that are no longer serving them or may even be holding them back. I want to help them make what they are hungering for become a reality. I want to help them know they are seen, are valued, and can make a difference in their lives.

It was after this workshop that Laura called me to ask if I would consider working with her, and I immediately said "Yes!" to helping her and Rick bring The Bigger Game work to the world.

In working on my bigger game, I had many conversations with Laura about what impact I wanted to have. Part of this was to help get the message of The Bigger Game out to many. I wanted to write a book for women to help inspire and motivate them as they searched for their compelling purpose; and I wanted to help support them on their journey to making that purpose a reality. Laura verbally agreed I could write a book focused on women. And so I began my work down this road.

Laura was diagnosed with lung cancer in 2005. She wrote about her journey on BlogSpot (http://www.laurawhitworth.blogspot.com). She openly shared what was happening in her life over the course of her illness, and did this in a very thoughtful and thought-provoking way. She knew that at this time in her life, her bigger game was fighting with all her power against cancer.

Throughout her illness, Laura was a tower of strength while showing what it is to simply be human. She was always bringing in elements of The Bigger Game model into her blog. "Allies," for example, is one of the nine elements of The Bigger Game model. Laura was a huge ally of mine. On April 1, she wrote about asking for support, which is what we all need to do to make our bigger games real. We can't do it alone; if we are, then it isn't a bigger game for us. Here is an excerpt from that blog:

> I just discovered, again, that I have sometimes felt shy about asking for your support, like there was something about me that was needy or helpless. Or that this may be going on too long and you will get tired and fed up and start tolerating or disappearing. And yet when I eventually find my feet, I realize what a natural yearning wanting support is for someone in my situation. And hopefully it is an opportunity for you. Maybe we don't need to have cancer to ask for support from each other. And maybe we don't need a reason to offer support to someone. What would that world be like, to know we will freely ask for support even when we haven't done anything to EARN it? And what a world it will be to take a moment each day and decide, who is the person(s) I want to send love or support or touch today. And do that. As a daily practice. Even a quick email or a post card. Hmmmm. That feels good to me. Receiving and Sending. What do you think? Thanks for listening. May you be enlivened by life.

Sixteen months later, on February 28, 2007, Laura passed away while en route home from receiving cancer treatments in Mexico. She was in a private plane with her partner in life and wife, Judy Pike. We said that at an altitude of 39,000 feet she was so close to heaven already the angels decided to take her right there, right then, in the sky, so she wouldn't have to travel so far.

After Laura's death, I dropped my book idea and the deep work with women. I continued to do a little bit of work with The Bigger Game, holding a few workshops and bringing the model into my work on an individual level. The intellectual property of The Bigger Game went to Rick Tamlyn's company, It's All Made Up. In 2014, I felt called again to pick up my work where I left it off many years ago. I did so with Rick's and his business partner Chuck Lioi's blessing to use the model as the basis of my book. What is most critical for Rick, just like me, is that the work be out and used in the world.

I write this book as a tribute to Laura. I want to keep this part of her life alive and moving forward. I want people to experience the impact of her work and be inspired to move forward in their lives. As I listen to women's stories and support and coach women on playing bigger games in their lives, the nine elements of the model keep popping out. I see over and over how this model can be applied and used as an everyday decision-making aid. This model pushes us toward answering a few compelling questions, such as: "Where do I consciously and with intention go next?" "What action is my bigger game calling me to take?" It's a place where you can look at where you've been, where you are now, and where you might step next.

The book in your hands will, I hope, inspire you through its presentation of stories about women who have become game changers in their worlds. These are women who realized they are here on Earth to be intentional about their impact in the world. Some, in essence, had their game find them. I hope that after reading their stories you will want more for yourself and those around you. That you will see your world needs you to be a game changer, a bigger game player, however you define this for yourself. That you will also know that now is the time. As the saying goes, "If not for you, who?"

As Diana Ross put it so boldly, "You can't just sit there and wait for people to give you that golden dream, you've got to get out there and make it happen yourself."

Let's get gutsy and get going.

Together.

Introduction

....

ARE YOU READY TO GET GUTSY AND GET GOING?

Gutsy \ GƏT-sē\ (adjective):

1. marked by courage, pluck, or determination; example: a gutsy fighter, a gutsy decision, a gutsy woman
2. expressing or characterized by basic physical senses or passions; example: gutsy macho talk, gutsy country blues, gutsy women win
3. YOU

This book is for you if you

- Have a burning desire for something bigger in your life;
- Know that where you are now is not fully using your one precious life;
- Take a look at the world around you and know, just know, that it must be different;
- Have a vision of something you want to do very differently from what you are doing now;
- Are feeling exhausted and burned out;
- Look around you and have a solution to solve a problem, but just don't know where to start;
- Feel your huge spirit and soul are slowly losing energy every single day and you just don't see a way out.

If you feel any of this list, you've picked up the right book. This is the beginning of playing a game bigger than anything you are doing right now. And by "bigger game" I simply mean that what you are up to in your life (the game) should excite and challenge you (the bigness). It's time for us, as women, to stop playing small, taking a back seat, limiting ourselves, and settling for less because it's safe.

It's time to get gutsy.

This is the beginning of making your own vision become a reality.

The book you have in your hands right now is different from the one that Laura Whitworth and Rick Tamlyn coauthored with Caroline Mac-Neill Hall in 2009, called *The Bigger Game: Why Playing a Bigger Game Designs Who You Want to Become.* That book is currently out of print.

Rick Tamlyn published *Play Your Bigger Game: 9 Minutes to Learn, a Lifetime to Live,* by Hay House, Inc. in 2013. This book delves deeply into the model itself and I recommend it if you want to do a deeper dive into the model.

Gutsy Women Win is a jump starter for you to become a game changer with a description of The Bigger Game model and examples of how this model has been used in my life, in some of my clients' lives, and in the lives of the women whose stories I tell. My vision is that this book and the stories in it will inspire you; it will answer the question "Why bother?" and help you find some part of yourself in each of the stories of women who have been playing big games in their lives and are going even bigger.

I know, I know. When you hear the words "a bigger game," you cringe. You say to yourself, "I don't want to play a bigger game. I'm already exhausted. I already have too much that is not getting done. I just can't fit this into my life. Maybe later." I'm here to tell you that playing your bigger game doesn't have to be hard. As a matter of fact, if it's hard, it's not the game you should be playing.

By "game" I simply mean what you're up to in life. Some of our games are conscious choices, such as choosing a college, selecting a career, or deciding to get married. Other games are games that we do not choose: getting fired or laid off, becoming seriously ill, or caring for ailing parents. These are all games that shape us, that make us who we are today. Who we have become is a result of these games.

There are many Bigger Games played out in business that have defined in essence who companies are. Apple produced the iPod, which changed the way we listen to music; the company sold 300 million units of this product in only ten years. In less than seven years, Virgin Airlines created a low-cost, customer-focused airline that remains number one in overall performance. Facebook changed the way we communicate with one another: At the end of 2015, Facebook had *1.59 billion* monthly active users, 864 million of whom are daily active users.

There are many Bigger Games in nonprofit organizations, too. The Global Fund for Women that was founded by Anne Firth Murray (you'll meet her in Chapter 7) has raised more than $100 million to help advance women's human rights. To help alleviate poverty, Kiva was founded to connect people through lending as little as $25.00. They have loaned in excess of $551 million with a repayment rate of 98.93 percent. Good360's mission is to fulfill the needs of nonprofits through corporate product donations.

These are all bigger games.

Don't let their "bigness" scare you away, though. Each of these games—just like The Bigger Game I'm teaching you—is "bigger" because it makes you bigger. It stretches you. It makes you go beyond your normal. It creates a "new" normal.

As Rick Tamlyn says, "The Bigger Game offers a philosophy and methodology for finding and releasing the full expression of your purpose and talents so that all of your years may be golden—and fun, too."

Imagine for a moment what kind of a person you would be if you released "the full expression of your purpose and talents"?

Oh yes, and fun, too. If it's not fun, why bother?

WOMEN I'VE ADMIRED

As I said in my tribute to Laura Whitworth, she was one of my heroes, mentors, coaches, and advisors. I've had many women who have supported me during my life. I have always admired these women for many different reasons, but mostly because they all modeled, in their own ways, the type of woman I wanted to become: strong, kind, a smart businesswoman, a good friend, ethical, and living my life by my strong values. Because of these women, I have become the woman I always wanted to be.

And in some ways, because of them, I have become even more than I imagined for myself.

Here are a few I'd like to mention.

My mother, Regina Slimkowski Obuchowski. My mother was one of the most kind and giving women I ever knew. We didn't have a lot of money growing up, and due to my dad being in a serious car accident when I was an infant, she had to work to make ends meet. I remember that she gave what extra money she had to her brother who had lost his job; to neighbors who just had their third baby and could hardly make the rent payment; and to a coworker who needed an advance to pay for a doctor for her sick husband. My mom was there for others, sacrificing to gladly help them. She simply thought it was the right thing to do, and that helping another human being in any way was the highest service there was. She taught me generosity and kindness.

Her Bigger Game: Spread kindness wherever she went.

My Aunt Jo, Josephine Lesniewski. My aunt and uncle were not able to have children in their lifetime, and for reasons I do not know, they never went through the adoption process. She loved children; I remember she donated to many children's organizations as well as volunteered at an orphanage.

As the youngest of three children—my sister and brother are older than me by ten and seven years respectively—I always felt a bit left out and left behind. When I came into the world, my parents had already done most of the "kid things" with my siblings. My Aunt Jo was the one adult in my life who made me feel special. I would spend the weekend at her home, where we would watch TV together and I could watch anything I wanted. She took me on my first visit to downtown Chicago, my first visit to the beach, my first visit to a restaurant, my first ride on a public bus, and my first ride on the Chicago elevated transit system. Sadly, she was also my first experience, at the age of thirteen, of the long illness and death of someone I loved.

Her Bigger Game: Make sure children are taken care of and know they are loved.

So many other women in my life play their Bigger Games and are game changers:

Laura Snow (Gawlik), my English teacher at Good Counsel High School. Miss Snow (I still can't call her by her first name) was the first teacher I had who was young and who I could easily identify with, especially since all my other teachers wore conventional nuns' habits. She had just graduated from college and this was her first teaching job. I always loved to read, but she brought into my space her love and enthusiasm for poetry and incorporated this into music. I used to sit in her class and listen to the poetry in musicians' songs, which led to a greater appreciation for musicians and lyricists.

Her Bigger Game: Teach everyone to appreciate the written word through a different perspective: poetry and music.

Katharine (Kate) Hepburn was an American actress in Hollywood for more than sixty years. She was known for her fierce independence and spirited personality. She received four Academy Awards for best actress, which is still a record for any performer. My view of Kate was that of one who shunned "business as usual" and refused to conform to society's expectations of women. She wore pants before it was common for women to do so. She was outspoken, assertive, and athletic. She led a very unconventional life and always played independent women in the movies. To me, she epitomized the type of woman I wanted to be. And let's not even speak about her forbidden twenty-six-year affair with her costar Spencer Tracy, which was hidden from the public.

Her Bigger Game: Living life on her terms.

Gloria Steinem is an American feminist, journalist, and social and political activist. She became nationally recognized as a leader and spokeswoman for the feminist movement in the late 1960s and 1970s. She was a columnist for *New York* magazine and a founder of *Ms.* magazine.

Gloria was the first woman I saw who spoke up for the equality of men and women. I viewed her as strong, intelligent, and inspiring and as providing the voice for those who felt they had no voice. She spoke up for what she believed in, regardless of the repercussions or criticism she received.

Her Bigger Game: To make women visible and have their voices heard.

Hillary Clinton is a former United States Secretary of State under President Barack Obama, US Senator (New York), and First Lady of the United States. Hillary personifies to me a woman who decides what the next bigger game is for herself and goes out and makes it happen. She made real for me the concept that "it takes a village." I carry this concept not just for raising children, but for most projects I get involved with. I cannot do it alone.

She was the Democratic nominee in the 2016 presidential election. I am hoping in my lifetime to witness the first woman to be elected president of the United States of America. Hillary was not the one. I still believe I will witness a woman become President.

Her Bigger Game (one of them): Encourage empowerment of women internationally.

Malala Yousafzai is the Pakistani schoolgirl who defied threats and was shot in the head by the Taliban for campaigning for the right for girls in her country to have access to education. She has become a global advocate for girls' and women's rights in education. She has received numerous peace awards and received the Nobel Peace Prize in 2014 along with Kailash Satyarthi, a children's rights activist in India.

Her Bigger Game: Ensure that all girls have a right to education.

As I reflect on these women, all from very different backgrounds, I notice that as they have moved through their lives and play(ed) the games they chose, they were all playing games that were bigger than the ones they played previously. Even though they did not consciously move through The Bigger Game model, I can point to areas in their lives and their games where they were using The Bigger Game pieces, and where they used the different game board pieces to make their life decisions. Some affected their direct communities and some affected the world.

You can, too. This book will help you find out how to get moving to create that Bigger Game that is waiting for you.

READING THE BOOK

In the first part of *Gutsy Women Win*, I explain The Bigger Gam and tell you the story of one of my intentional Bigger Games. Ch helps you get a high-level understanding of what this model is a ut. I step you through the game board in a linear manner. I have also included a few questions for each game piece to ask yourself as you are working on determining the answers to your own Bigger Game.

In Chapter 2, I share one of my intentional Bigger Games, which was creating the largest women's conference in my county, and how I used The Bigger Game to help me create something from nothing and have it be very successful.

I have used this model with great success with individuals and organizations I've worked with. I'll give you a few examples.

I also explain how I use the model to help me see where I am right now and where I need to go. I use it to make everyday decisions about which direction would be the best for me to choose and what resources I need.

In the second part of the book, you will meet seven women I've interviewed who have inspired me. These women represent business, politics, and agriculture, to name a few segments. They all come from diverse backgrounds educationally, culturally, in their careers, and in the ways they were raised.

I chose these women because of their diverse lives and bigger games. They inspired me and I'm confident they will do the same for you.

What they all have in common is that they are playing a bigger game. They didn't know about The Bigger Game model, but when I saw what they were up to in the world and what they had accomplished, I related each story to the pieces of the model. All these women agreed that looking back on their journey, they could see how their decisions and actions were reflected in the game pieces. They could also see how it would serve as a valuable tool for deciding which direction to go in next.

The conclusion shares my vision and an invitation to you, my reader, to join the Gutsy Women Win movement. It's a place where you can find resources, support, and community to make your bigger game a reality. We'll support you as you change your world for the better.

If you are interested in contacting the women featured in this book, you can go to www.GutsyWomenWin.com, where you will find contact information for each of the seven interviewees.

GET GUTSY!

Let's get you started.

As Laura Whitworth used to say, "People want to make a difference in the world; they just don't know how. We're here to show them how."

As Rick Tamlyn says, "The Bigger Game takes nine minutes to learn and a lifetime to live."

As I say, "Let's get gutsy and get going. Together."

Chapter 1

LEARNING THE BIGGER GAME MODEL GAME BOARD

What I present in this chapter is a brief explanation of The Bigger Game model, along with a few reflective questions to guide you on your journey. This model came to life with the purpose of having a common language between individuals who want to become more aware, alive, and insightful—not only *finding* their purpose, but also *making it real* in the world. And then not only *making it real* in the world, but also *finding their tribe* to help, guide, and join them along the way.

So let's take The Bigger Game cofounder and author Rick Tamlyn at his word and spend nine minutes to learn the model so you can start, today, to live it for the rest of your life.

"PLAY A BIGGER GAME" DEFINED

Let's take the three key words and define them:

- **"Play"** As I think of defining this, I think about when I was a child and spent a lot of my time playing. Simply doing the things I thought were fun. It was simply having that sense of wonder and spontaneity and curiosity that brought me enormous joy. It was doing the things that were easy and effortless to do. As an adult, I find that those two traits—easy and effortless—continue to bring me joy. I am not saying your bigger game will always be easy and effortless, but if you think about it in the context of having fun, isn't that what we want to do in life? To play? To have more fun in our lives? Bring back that sense of wonder and spontaneity and curiosity? Isn't that what we want more of? Your bigger game can be fun. As a matter of fact, it needs to be. Otherwise, why bother?

- **"Bigger"** This simply means what you do is a stretch for you. It is challenging and helps you grow and learn. In my coaching work, quite a few of my clients leave their employers because they are not being challenged, nor do they think they are having the impact they want to have. I frequently hear clients say: "I'm playing too small."

- **"Game"** This just means what you are up to in your life; where you spend your resources; what you are doing to make a difference. We are playing different games all the time. The College Game, the Marriage Game, the Parent Game, the Divorce Game—and, for some of us, the Marriage Game a second time. It is simply what game we decide to play at this particular time in our lives. Notice what I just said: "It is simply what game we *decide* to play." The operative word here is "decide."

Your choice to do it or not.

Your choice to play big or not.

Doesn't putting yourself in the service of something you deeply care about, getting a little bit scared about doing something you haven't done before, sound like "playing" and "bigger" and a "game"?

The Bigger Game is a model where you make a conscious decision about what direction you want your days, weeks, months, years, and entire life to go. It is about living with intention and challenging yourself to move forward in making the difference you want to make in your world.

It is not just about you any longer.

It is about something bigger.

Playing your bigger game will be life altering if you allow it to be.

Reflective Questions

Are you ready to play a bigger game? An answer of "yes" to any of these questions will tell you that you are.

- Are you ready to have a more positive impact on your family, your work, your community, or your workplace?
- Do you yearn for more meaningful work that truly matters— work where you are using your strengths?
- Do you hunger for a change in your life, or feel a nudge for something different, but you are not sure what it is?
- Do you want to take responsibility for your life and stop feeling like a victim?
- Do you aspire to make a difference or leave a legacy in your lifetime?
- Are you ready to step up and be a leader to those who need you to be? They are waiting.

A "BIGGER GAME PLAYER" DEFINED

You. A Game Changer.

I'm pretty sure you are already a Bigger Game Player who is expressing your purpose in some way. You picked up this book, so you must want to stretch yourself, but you may not know what's next. Hopefully this will help you find that for yourself.

THE PIECES OF THE BIGGER GAME DEFINED

I know you may not be familiar with the model. That is exactly why I want you to look at the game board now, without knowing how these pieces are defined. Just take a look.

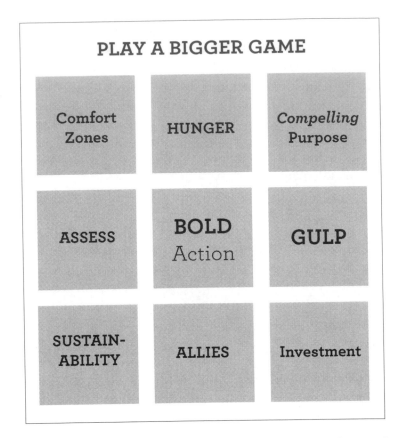

Now let me ask: "If you imagine this board laid on the floor in front of you, where would you choose to stand? Which piece of this game board draws you to it?"

I bet that the piece you chose on the board—maybe even more than one—parallels where you are right now in your game.

I ask you this question before even defining the pieces because I believe we are at all times in our lives in at least one of these squares. Right now, editing this book, I am in a few of the squares. I am on the Hunger piece, as I have the hunger to complete this book. This book is one of the bigger games I am playing right now. I am also in the Assess piece, as I am assessing the words on this page to ensure that my message is understandable, and also thinking of how I will market it. I am also in the Allies piece, as I can hear my editor, Linda O'Doughda, making suggestions, encouraging me, and supporting this game of mine.

All I'm saying here is that there are many, many ways to approach this game board. Refer to this model throughout the day and see how easily your position changes based on the present moment.

For the sake of your learning and understanding, I've presented the nine pieces going clockwise, beginning with Comfort Zones and ending in the center with Bold Action. But the model is not a linear model. As you experienced in the game board earlier, you can be in any one piece or many pieces of the game board at any one time. You can approach this game board in many different ways. It has been my and my clients' experience that we can approach the game board in a very logical manner if needed, especially when trying to really get a grasp on exactly what bigger game we want to consciously pursue at this time in our lives. I felt like I had to leave quite a few comfort zones before I could even look at what my hunger or compelling purpose was. One of the comfort zones I left was how much I needed to know *how* I was going to do everything.

Some people approach the game board according to a logical or practical order. They prioritize according to which pieces, in their estimation, would serve as the foundation for the other pieces—the idea that "I must do this before I can do that." As an example, one might assess and gather allies before they take a bold action. One may determine how they are able to sustain themselves before they can take a GULP and then take bold action.

One note of warning as you go step by step through the game board: When you're looking at what your game is, don't look yet at *"How* do I do this?" Stay with *"Why* does this need to happen?" Don't listen to that voice that tries to creep in with the "how" to do it, as it can then become so overwhelming you're tempted to give up. Tell that voice, also known as the saboteur, gremlin, or monkey mind: "You'll have your time later." And it will. The how will be explained later. For now, let yourself be creative in your thinking, and keep looking at the possibilities.

Let's travel across the game board and reflect on the nine pieces.

Comfort Zones

Comfort Zones are the habits we have—neither good nor bad—that we need to be aware of, because they may be preventing us from playing our bigger game. Comfort Zones may be keeping us in the same old place, as they are just that—they are comfortable. And who wants to leave a place that is comfortable for what is unknown and more than likely uncomfortable?

A Comfort Zone can be a behavior or an action of some sort. For instance, how many of us watch too much TV, are on our smartphones way too much, work too many hours, fill our time up with busy work, or procrastinate? How many of us worry endlessly, are agreeable all the time, avoid confrontation, fear commitment to something, or avoid change? Pursuing comfort is just what we do as human beings. We don't like change, and we like to be comfortable. A Comfort Zone is a very safe place to hang around in and to just be.

How many of us spend our time being safe doing what we're good at and getting kudos without challenging ourselves? How many of us just get by doing the least we can do without doing what we know we are really capable of doing?

Several years ago, I sought the advice of a career counseling company. I had been a full-time employee in the business world, working in the technology arena. At that time, I was looking for another job with another company in the same field. It was suggested to me by my career counselor that I attend a workshop for entrepreneurship. I thought, "Why not?" The facilitator said something to me that I'll never forget: "Don't look for the same type of work that you've been doing just because you are good at it and you know how to do it. Open up your possibilities and your perspective, and take a look at what you may never have looked at before. Don't let the 'I don't know how' stop you from just looking."

These were the words that had me examine my future through a different lens. I opened up to a different perspective and I got in touch with my Why. One of the things I loved most about all my leadership positions inside organizations was developing my teams, as individuals and as teams, focusing on results together, and integrating our whole selves into our work. Looking into wanting to support and encourage leaders to focus on their impact and building great teams helped me land on my current work as an executive and leadership coach in my own successful business for over fifteen years.

I did not worry about the "how" until I fully understood my "why." Then the "how" wasn't so overwhelming.

The thing about Comfort Zones is that they need to be examined frequently. Unexamined Comfort Zones—namely, those routines and habits that keep us in a "business as usual" mode—can run our lives.

We need to take a good look at our Comfort Zones to determine whether *they* are running us or *we* are running them. A Comfort Zone that no longer supports us or who we want to be fuels our inertia. If it is moving us toward apathy, decay, or chronic ambivalence, it is time to leave it and move on. Turn off the TV. Turn off the laptop. Pick up the phone. Ask for help. We need to leave our Comfort Zones for the sake of feeding our Hunger and living our Compelling Purpose.

One of my Comfort Zones is the need to know everything before I can make a decision and move forward. Sometimes this prevents me from taking a bold action because I won't take that action unless I have all those ducks in a row. You can see how this Comfort Zone would—and let me assure you, it does—stop me from moving forward sooner, *every time!*

I've given you just a few representative examples of what a Comfort Zone can be. You need to be able to leave your specific Comfort Zones that are no longer serving you in order to move forward, because if you are comfortable with the game you are presently playing, it is not a Bigger Game. You already know how to play that game, and you're ready to start something new.

Reflection

- What are some Comfort Zones that serve me, are good for me, and help me?

- What are some Comfort Zones that stop me from moving forward in my Bigger Game?

- What are the rewards I have for sitting tight in this piece?

- If I leave this Comfort Zone, what better opportunities or possibilities are out there for me?

- What is one thing I can do today, right now, even a small action that would help me let go of a Comfort Zone that is holding me back?

Hunger

Let's stand in the Hunger piece, together. To hunger is to want. As adults, wanting is not really valued in our society. We don't let ourselves want, let alone want deeply, due to our fear of failure or of being disappointed. As Rick Tamlyn says, "If we don't want much, we won't be disappointed." Disappointment seems to be the last place that we want to visit. Because of this fear, we don't even begin the journey.

We start out dreaming, as children and young adults, of what we will do when we grow up and what difference we will make in the world, but somewhere along our lifeline, we begin letting go of these dreams. The story I consistently hear is "I have to be practical." We feel we must get a good job, support our families, have more things, obtain what our neighbors have, etc. This gets us into the comfort zones that we don't want to leave because, well, of course, they become comfortable.

Hunger is the piece you stand in when you feel a desire for something more, even if you have no idea what that something is. This is where you begin to think about what you're hungering for, and what the world hungers for that you might provide.

Ever since I was a little girl, I always felt that there was a difference in the way boys and girls were treated. I had a hunger to do and have things that were very clearly (as my parents and teachers and even girlfriends reminded me) boys' activities and toys. I think I had a hunger then to be able to be the same as boys and play the same games and have the same toys. As I grew older and chose business as my career, I found out very quickly about gender inequality in this arena. It was here that I began feeding this hunger of gender equality in the world and became involved in many different women's organizations that had gender equality as their goal.

We talk about looking at our Hunger through three different lenses. As you get in touch with your own Hunger, look through each of these:

- "No, not that." For example, one could say "No, not that" to war and begin working in the peace movement. I said "No, not that" when I became actively involved in several professional women's organizations that had the goal of gender equality.

- "Yes. More of that." For example, something may be working and we take a look at it and say, "Wow, I want more of that." I said, "Yes. More of that" when I was appointed to the Commission on the Status of Women. I knew there were some aspects of gender equality that were working in the legislative arena, so I said I wanted to work there. "Yes! More of that."

- "Something is missing." For example, we take a look around and we see a big black hole where no one is doing anything. "That is what's missing." I said "Something is missing" when I realized that women need to learn the skills and have support to take risks and create big things in their lives. I researched this and heard from both men and women that this was missing for women in today's society. This was missing for me. "Something is missing," and the "Gutsy Women Win" movement was created.

As you can see in the examples above, my hunger focused in each of these lenses at different times in my life. When you are connecting with your hunger, when you are questioning what you are really hungry for in your world, you may see your hunger through one, or two, or even all three lenses.

Hunger feeds our game. Hunger is a powerful desire for something more. It is the fire that keeps us engaged and fulfilled and living the lives we are meant to live. Staying connected to our hunger is what keeps us, and our game, going. When you feel you can't go on playing your bigger game, get back in touch with your hunger.

When I begin to think that the work I'm doing is not having the impact I want and maybe I should give it up, I begin talking to other women and ask them what some of their challenges are. In these conversations, I am always brought back to my hunger.

I keep up to date on local and world affairs and see the inequality women experience everywhere because they don't have the skills or the confidence to use their voice, nor do they have support to encourage them.

Reconnect with your hunger by going back to the reason you began your game. Connect with the people you are serving and you'll connect with your hunger again. You will remember.

There will come a time when a game you are playing may morph or perhaps even play to its end. This will be a time to go back and look at the three lenses of hunger; it will be a time to begin thinking about another Bigger Game to play, because once you've awakened the hunger in you, there is no turning back.

Steve Jobs, Apple's cofounder, gave a legendary commencement speech at Stanford. In this speech he spoke about the end of a very popular catalog at the time called "Whole Earth." They published their final issue in the mid-1970s. On the back cover of this final issue was a photograph of an early morning country road. Beneath it were the words "Stay hungry. Stay foolish." It was their final sign-off. Jobs said, "I've always wished this for myself."

This is my wish for you, too. "Stay hungry. Stay foolish."

Reflection

- What does my soul want for the world? What do I want to see changed?
- What am I really dissatisfied with?
- What am I excited about creating more of?
- What do I hunger for in my professional life?
- What do I hunger for in my personal life?

Compelling Purpose

Compelling Purpose is all about what you are here to do in this life and how you want to be used. What drives you? What is inside you that keeps you going? Compelling Purpose works on a more personal level than Hunger does. It is more about turning inward and looking at "me." It is that place of deep knowing.

This is your vision of what must happen in the world. It's that place that answers the questions "What am I truly about?" and "What do I stand for?" This is where you feel you are being pulled toward something. It is your purpose that is compelling you to move and take action.

As I spoke about in the Hunger section above, the hunger I feel is to have gender equality worldwide. My compelling purpose is personal. I want women to use their voices to speak up for themselves and know they make a difference in the world.

Early in my career, I introduced myself to a new vice president in the company I was working for. He was male. I walked into his office, where he was leaning back in his chair with his feet on his desk. I extended my hand for a handshake and said, "How do you do? I'm Pat Obuchowski."

He turned slowly and looked at me. He did not stand to reciprocate the handshake. He looked at me; up, and then down, and then back up again for a few seconds. Then he said, "Don't you mean, *who* do I do?"

I was stunned. I stood there with my hand out and felt my eyes widening. I forgot to breathe. No, I couldn't breathe. I felt like I had no voice to tell him what I was feeling. When I finally caught my breath, I just laughed nervously and said, "Nice to meet you." I turned around and walked away. In some way, I felt ashamed for something that was clearly not my fault.

I don't want any woman to feel this way. I want her to be the kind of woman I wanted to be at that moment, but didn't have the self-confidence or guts to be. I want women to speak up and say, "Not acceptable! Not now! Not ever!"

This is my compelling purpose. This is very personal to me.

Because we have complex lives and many things touch us, we may have more than one compelling purpose. Take them all out and look at what has the most resonance for you. What has the strongest pull? When you tap into your compelling purpose it feels deeply satisfying and fulfilling.

Find your compelling purpose. When you do, become aware of the synchronicities that begin to happen in your life. These are the occurrences—that appear to be coincidences—that help you play your Bigger Game. Trust me, they will begin to happen!

Reflection

- What do I wish was different in the world?
- What would I change if I had a magic wand?
- What injustice(s) exist in my workplace or community or even in the world?
- What must change?
- What is the impact I long to have in my life?
- What is my legacy?
- Is my compelling purpose strong enough to lead me to examine the comfort zones that are not serving me? Does it lead me to examine the comfort zones that are stopping me from being a game changer?

GULP

You know you have moved over into the GULP piece when you take a look at your hunger, compelling purpose, and the work that has to be done in the world, and you get a little bit afraid. Or maybe a lot.

When you take a look at what it is you want to do, it feels "GULP-y." You start asking yourself, "Who am I to think I can do this?" And then you answer with such protests as "I'm too old; I'm too young; I don't speak in public very well; I don't have enough education; I don't have enough money; I don't have enough experience; I've never done anything like this before; I've . . ." Add whatever your excuses are that stop you cold.

You also know you are in the GULP piece whenever you decide you are going to leave a comfort zone. All of a sudden you're in unfamiliar territory and it feels "GULP-y."

I love this feeling. To me it is just like that scary exhilaration you feel when you are slowly climbing to the top of an arc on a roller coaster. You feel anxious and excited and scared all rolled into one. At the top, you stop for a split second—GULP—then *whoosh!* You are on your way down and just enjoying the ride, screaming at the top of your lungs and laughing like you rarely laugh.

Think about a time when you were heading into unfamiliar territory. Perhaps you were giving a presentation that was really important. Perhaps you walked into your boss's office to ask for a raise. Perhaps you walked into your workplace on your first day of work.

Do you remember that feeling? Butterflies in the stomach? Not completely sure you were doing the right thing? Wishing you were somewhere else? That is the GULP.

I had that feeling when I left my hometown of Chicago, Illinois, at the age of twenty-five to move to San Francisco, California.

I had that feeling when I decided to go back for my master's degree while holding a full-time job.

I had that feeling when I began to ask investors to invest $250,000 in my business.

I have this feeling when I start anything new that really matters to me.

When you are on the GULP piece, risk is always a factor. Failure is always a distinct possibility. But like I say, "Feel the GULP and do it anyway."

And remember: if you don't feel GULP along the way, it's not a bigger game for you.

Reflection

- How would I describe the GULP feeling?
- What were some lifetime experiences when I felt the GULP?
- What have I done recently that was "GULP-y" for me?
- What is stopping me from purposefully experiencing more GULPs?
- What would my life be like if I felt "GULP-y" regularly, and I loved it?

Investment

Let's head into the Investment piece. By investment, I mean the things that you, as a game changer, have to invest in to make your game real. The investment has to be a stretch of some sort. Perhaps it's an investment of your time or money. It may be an investment of some educational or professional development training. You may need this to fill in the gap of something that you don't know how to do.

The investment piece is about what we need to invest—time or money, or what we need to learn, or what new skills we need to acquire to have our Bigger Game become a reality. If we want to be an author, we need to learn about publishing or marketing. If we want to create a nonprofit, we need to learn how to legally set one up or how to do fundraising. If we want to run for a political office, we may need to learn Campaigning 101 or how to network effectively.

This piece is also about committing our time. Yes, playing a bigger game often takes a great deal of time. Two questions I ask myself when I am looking at where to invest my time are: "Is this the best use of me?" and "Will this forward my game?" If I answer no to either one, I probably won't do it.

This piece is also sometimes about investing your money. This could take the form of raising money to start a business or by taking classes or workshops to learn a new skill. You may need to be sure your finances are in order.

The most important aspect of investment is investing in you. It's investing to be the best you can be for the sake of your game and keeping it and you fully alive and thriving. This can take the form of saying "no" to things you used to say "yes" to.

Reflection

When I think of my Bigger Game, what do I need in terms of:

- Skills?
- Time?
- Money?
- What must change in my life to allow me to obtain the above?
- What must I do to invest in myself for the sake of my game?

Allies

Let's drop next door onto the Allies piece.

The good news about playing a Bigger Game is that you don't have to do it by yourself. Not only that, you *cannot* do it by yourself because it is not a bigger game if you do. That would make it a self game.

The allies you have in your life can be your supporters; the champions who support you in your game or the cheerleaders who voice their encouragement. They might be co-players too; someone who is right alongside you playing the same game.

Naysayers can also be good allies. How? Because when a naysayer says, "You can't do that," your response is probably, "I'll show you that I can." Naysayers help you stiffen your resolve and are capable of pointing out some possible pitfalls. Listen to them.

Other allies could be your employer, your family and friends, Mother Nature, or your pets. In other words, most anybody or anything that inspires you and helps keep you moving forward is your ally.

We must purposefully design our relationships with our Bigger Game allies. This means that we communicate clearly how we want others to support us. Perhaps we need a co-player in our game. Perhaps we need a group of allies to brainstorm with us. We can even find allies who can hold us accountable. People want to help. Let them.

One Buddhist definition of suffering is forgetting we are all connected. Joy is remembering that we are all connected. This gives you the opportunity as a game changer to remind others we are all connected—and you need them to connect with you in specific ways. Perhaps you are the one person in someone's life who helps show him or her how to engage in a Bigger Game. Ask such a person to help. This person is waiting for you.

Laura Whitworth used to say of coaching: "I believe every person wants to make a difference in the world. They just don't know how. We're here to show them." After many years of being involved in learning about human potential and behavior, coaching others, and playing quite a few bigger games, I, too, believe in her words.

Reflection

- Who are some allies who would support my Bigger Game and me?
- Who might be co-players with me?
- Who are my champions I can connect with when I feel overwhelmed?
- Who are my naysayers and how can they become my allies?
- What expert resources can be allies?
- What allies can I find in a spiritual community, in nature, from my pets?
- What allies can hold me accountable to my Bigger Game?

Sustainability

The next square is Sustainability. This piece is about our ability to sustain ourselves so we can give the best to our games. Living a balanced life is crucial to playing your bigger game.

Sustainability is taking care of your needs to keep yourself going. It is getting enough sleep, eating well, having playtime to reenergize, connecting to your spirituality (however you define it), spending time with family and friends, playing with pets, and being financially stable. It is about keeping *you* healthy—physically, mentally, emotionally, spiritually.

If you can't sustain yourself, you can't sustain your game. It is that simple. But the beautiful reward is that your bigger game itself will help sustain you and give you energy.

Your game demands that you take superb care of yourself. If you are feeling exhausted, tired, or burned out, then you need to ask yourself, "Is this the right game for me?" When we sell out, who is the first person we sell out on? Ourselves.

No sustainability = no game changer.

If you're not sustaining yourself in whatever ways you most need to do, start right now.

There is another part to this game piece. It's not just about you; it is also about the game you are playing. This part deals with being able to sustain the impact of your bigger game so it endures and serves as a legacy. If you choose legacy as a part of your game, the game should be designed so that if you were to leave it by choice or because of some life circumstance beyond your control, it could sustain itself. The Bigger Game could and should be able to go on without us.

Reflection

- What do I need to start doing for the sake of my bigger game?
- What do I need to stop doing for the sake of my bigger game?
- What are three things I need to do right now to provide me with sustainability?
- What do I need to do to ensure that what I'm building will endure beyond me?

Assess

It's time to move back up to the second row, where we'll visit the Assess piece. Every now and then we need to take a look at our game and assess how we are doing. We are assessing all the time. This just means that we evaluate, gauge, estimate, consider, and analyze what is occurring in our lives. We assess our own lives all the time.

We assess our relationships. Am I in the right relationship? What kind of relationships do I want to have with my children? What needs to change in my relationships with my friends?

We assess our careers. Shall I stay in this career? What do I need to do to prepare myself for a promotion? What type of company do I really want to work at? Am I happy in my career?

We assess our health. Do I need to exercise more? Do I need to change my eating habits? What can I do to control my stress level? Am I getting enough sleep?

These are just a few areas in our life that we assess frequently. After we assess, we then determine what direction would be best for us to head into. What needs to change? What needs to remain the same?

We must ask ourselves questions that take into consideration virtually all of the other Bigger Game pieces:

- Am I still playing the right game?
- Am I doing the things that keep my game moving forward?
- Am I still investing in myself and the right things?
- Do I have the right allies?
- Am I leaving the comfort zones that I must to really make my game a reality?
- Do I need to change something?
- Am I sustaining myself?

Businesses regularly inventory their goods and evaluate their financial strength to determine if they are heading in the right direction or need to make adjustments. As with any goal we set, we need to take a look at our progress. What are the key results we want to achieve? How will we achieve them? By when do we need to achieve them? Who can help us achieve them?

As game changers, we must learn to assess where we are in relationship to the game plan. The key is to do this without judging. I know this is harder than it sounds, but we need to keep trying to look objectively (as much as possible) at where we are in moving our game forward.

Above all else, we need to constantly assess ourselves and our hunger and compelling purpose. Do these still drive us? Do these still feed us? If not, it may be time to morph the game into something else, or even to let the game go.

One of my bigger games that I mentioned earlier was being appointed to the Commission on the Status of Women in San Mateo County, California. I served on the executive board, including the position of president. I served two terms and was up for reappointment for a third term. The Board of Supervisors would have easily appointed me again due to the results of my work. At that time, I assessed where I was and the impact I was having on the commission. I decided that after six years I was no longer looking at the issues through the lens of possibilities. I did not feel that my future contributions to the board would be as valuable as opening the position up to someone with new eyes and a different viewpoint. I just felt my time was complete with what I wanted to achieve and the mark I wanted to make. It was time to let go and focus my energies on another bigger game.

Was this a failure? Not at all. I just assessed my situation and made the decision that it was not the best use of me at that time.

Another bigger game I played was to help advance the profession of coaching. When I left my full-time job and made my choice to start my own business in the field of coaching in 2001, it was a very young profession. I decided to join the International Coach Federation, the international accrediting and credentialing body for the coaching profession. Coming from a business background, I believed it was extremely important that this profession be credible in the business world. When I assessed how I could help do this, I decided I wanted to help define ethics for the profession, so I became a member of the Ethics Committee. When we had finished revising the Code of Ethics for the organization, I assessed what I wanted to do next. I decided I wanted to help build community and joined the Membership Committee. I then became chair of the Special Interest Group Committee and then Membership chair. After that, I decided to apply for the International Board of Directors and was voted by the membership to serve on the Board.

As you can see, my bigger game of helping to advance the profession of coaching morphed into serving on one committee and then to serving on the International Board. Along the way, I kept assessing where I was and where I wanted to go next.

When Wes Moore, author of *The Work: Searching for a Life That Matters*, was asked why he wrote the book, he replied, "I remember going through this evolution. I wanted to find what it meant to be successful. What did all this really mean in my own life? And in this quest and this journey, my understanding of the work really became where your greatest gifts and your greatest skill sets begin to start overlapping with the world's greatest needs and then you choose to do something about it."

That is where you find your compelling purpose.

Games get created. They morph. They finish. Games begin anew.

Reflection

- What do I need to make my game real?

- How do I make mine a sustainable bigger game?

- Am I fully engaged in the game? Do I need to just recharge, or start looking elsewhere?

- What may be holding me back from clearly assessing my game?

- What allies can I ask to help me assess my game objectively?

Bold Action

Let's dive into the middle of the game board. The center piece of the model is Bold Action. The operative word here is BOLD. It is in the middle of the game board because it takes Bold Action to be actively, consciously, and intentionally in any one of the other pieces. You don't plan for boldness; it happens because you are pulled into action.

For instance—

- It takes bold action to look around and know that something must change and you are the only one to be the catalyst for that change, because you are actively in touch with your hunger and compelling purpose.

- It takes bold action to leave your comfort zones for the sake of your game. When I was in the middle of playing a game of growing a business with a partner, we decided that to take our business to the next level, we needed an inflow of cash. We needed to find an investor. When I worked in large companies, I learned to negotiate and received approval for multimillion-dollar projects. This was different. Asking for money for my business was like asking for money for me. This made it very personal. I had a comfort zone around not asking for money if it was personal. This was a comfort zone I had to examine and decide to leave in order to grow the business. (By the way, we did find an investor.)

- It takes bold action to be in the GULP piece. This is the place where excitement and fear feel like the same thing. This is the place that is described in the quote by author Susan Jeffers, "Feel the fear and do it anyway." Why in the world would anyone do this by choice? Because this is the place that is exciting. This is the place where you know you can be a positive force for change. I felt that GULP when I had to ask the investors for money to invest in my business. It was a very scary place to be, but also the most rewarding as I was handed a check for more than $250,000 (over $400,000 in today's dollars).

- Bold Action is needed while you're in the Investment piece. This is where you need to really plan what resources you need to create, run, and sustain your bigger game. This is where you need to plan for the investments of time, money, learning, effort, etc.

- It takes bold action to find allies. As I said earlier, I was the youngest of three children with seven years' difference between my brother and me, and ten years' difference between my sister and me. This age gap taught me to be independent at a very early age. Because my siblings always shooed me aside, I also learned to not ask for help and to figure things out by myself. These can be good skills and can come in handy, but when you are planning to really play a bigger game, you can't do it by yourself. You need to find allies. I have found that playing a bigger game with allies is so much more fun than doing anything by yourself.

- Sustainability is another bold action. Here is where you need to stop and assess what you need to do to take care of yourself and keep your game moving forward. When I left the Board of Directors for the International Coach Federation, I had spent ten years volunteering for this organization. I was complete and burned out on my work with them. I needed to leave to sustain me.

As Rick Tamlyn says, "This is about taking action that is beyond 'business as usual.'"

Take a moment to look back at the image of the model at the beginning of this chapter. If you were to move onto any piece on the game board now, what would be a bold move for you?

When you take bold action, the world knows you are up to something big. You are no longer playing small. Your bigger game won't let you.

Reflection

- For the sake of my game, what do I need to boldly ask for?
- For the sake of my game, whom do I need to boldly ask?
- Where do I let fear get in the way of my boldness?
- Whom do I need to ask to keep me accountable to being bold for the sake of my game?

WHO ARE YOU BECOMING?

The Bigger Game model stands on this foundation: *The size and quality of the game you play designs who you are becoming.* We are always becoming and changing into someone who is different today from the person we were yesterday. The Bigger Game model provides us with a guide to become more conscious of our next step in becoming the person we have the potential to be.

The model will help you get to a more conscious level in understanding that you are living with intention and designing who you are becoming. If you play your Bigger Game, who do you imagine you'll be in the coming year? What type of a game changer will you be?

Who are you becoming?

Chapter 2

·················

MY FIRST (INTENTIONAL) BIGGER GAME

A poem by Marianne Williamson hangs in my office and moves with me wherever my office may go.

> Our deepest fear is not that we are inadequate. Our deepest fear is that we are powerful beyond measure. It is our light, not our darkness, that most frightens us. We ask ourselves, who am I to be brilliant, gorgeous, talented, and fabulous? Actually, who are you not to be? You are a child of God. Your playing small doesn't serve the world. We were born to make manifest the glory of God that is within us. It's not just in some of us; it's in everyone. And as we let our own light shine, we unconsciously give other people permission to do the same. As we are liberated from our own fear, our presence automatically liberates others.

These words particularly move me into action: "We ask ourselves, who am I to be brilliant, gorgeous, talented, and fabulous? Actually, who are you *not* to be?" (Emphasis added.)

Whenever I read this I feel there is a finger pointing at me saying, "If you are not brilliant, gorgeous, talented, and fabulous, you are cheating us all out of possibilities; you are falling short of making things real and coming into being." This book is about becoming brilliant, gorgeous, talented, empowered, impactful, and fabulous. This book is about becoming a bigger game player, a bigger game leader, and a game changer. "Who are you *not* to be?"

I wrote *Gutsy Women Win* because I know how rewarding it is to live and play a game that is intentional. I know how much fun it is to develop and evolve into something I never imagined. I know how amazing it is to watch a bigger game that I'm involved with develop and become a reality. I know the joy of having a hunger to help others do this too.

I also know the impact I have when others watch me being a game changer. "*As we are liberated from our own fear, our presence automatically liberates others.*"

Remember, as I said earlier, when I use the word "game," I merely mean what you are up to in this life. I think the greatest question we as human beings should ponder is "What is my purpose in life?" Or, asked in a different way: "What the heck am I doing here?"

As I described in the tribute to Laura Whitworth that opens this book, I traveled to London a few years ago to participate in a three-day workshop called "The Bigger Game." I didn't have any great revelations during that weekend, nor did I see a clear path for what I was to do and who I was to be. But it did give me some juicy material to think over and reflect on. I knew something had shifted in the way I thought about myself, those in my life, and even humanity at large. I also knew something had shifted in the way I wanted to interact with and be in the world. If anything, the workshop got me more in touch with my humanness and the recognition that I must live my life with intention and consciousness.

Those three days also brought me to a place where I realized it was no longer all about me. In my leadership coaching business, I discuss in depth with my clients the importance of "servant" leadership. This phrase was coined by Robert K. Greenleaf, who was the founder of the modern Servant Leadership movement and the Greenleaf Center for Servant Leadership. In 1970, he published his first essay, entitled "The Servant as Leader," which first introduced the term "servant leadership."

> The servant-leader *is* servant first. It begins with the natural feeling that one wants to serve, to serve *first*. Then

conscious choice brings one to aspire to lead. That person is sharply different from one who is *leader* first, perhaps because of the need to assuage an unusual power drive or to acquire material possessions. For such it will be a later choice to serve—after leadership is established. The leader-first and the servant first are two extreme types. Between them there are shadings and blends that are part of the infinite variety of human nature.

The difference manifests itself in the care taken by the servant-first to make sure that other people's highest priority needs are being served. The best test, and difficult to administer, is: Do those served grow as persons? Do they, *while being served*, become healthier, wiser, freer, more autonomous, more likely themselves to become servants? *And*, what is the effect on the least privileged in society? Will they benefit or at least not be further deprived?

It can't be all about you if you want to make a difference. You do not move in your world without coming in contact with others. You cannot better your world without bettering others, and vice versa. It's that old adage "We're in this together," and The Bigger Game model reminded me of that and pushed me in the direction of "Don't you forget it." It was also a very strong affirmation that we belong to one another.

I was looking at the hunger that was waking up in me. That hunger was to see more kindness in a world where I believe people are no longer as kind to one another as they once were. I have always had a strong feeling that all people must be seen and heard; they need to know they make a difference. This "seeing" and "hearing" others is one of my definitions of kindness.

How many times have we asked someone "How are you?" hoping that we don't get more than a one-word response such as "Fine" or "Good"? How often do we just continue to walk on and not stop to acknowledge the person answering—or perhaps asking—the question, just so we'll be able to continue with whatever we were doing with minimal disruption?

How does it make you feel to not be acknowledged or to be brusquely brushed off or completely ignored?

For me, there is a depth of validation for each other as human beings that is missing in our current world.

I have often wondered how other cultures greet each other. I found that among the tribes of northern KwaZulu-Natal in South Africa, the most common greeting that is equivalent to "hello" in English is the expression "Sawa Bona." It means, "I see you," as if to say, "I respect and acknowledge you for who you are." If you are a member of one of the tribes you might reply, "Sikbona," which means, "I am here," as if to say, "When you see me, you bring me into existence." The order of the exchange is important: until you see me I do not exist.

This meaning, implicit in the language, is part of the spirit of *ubuntu*, a frame of mind prevalent among native peoples in sub-Saharan Africa. The word *ubuntu* stems from the folk saying, "Umuntu ngumuntu ngabantu," which, from Zulu, literally translates as "A person is a person because of other people." If you grow up with this perspective, your identity is based upon the fact that you are seen; that the people around you respect and acknowledge you as a person.

During the last few years in South Africa, many corporations have begun to employ managers who were raised in the tribal regions. The ubuntu ethic often clashes subtly with the culture of those corporations. In an office, for instance, it's perfectly normal to pass someone in the hall, while preoccupied, and not greet them. This would be worse than a sign of disrespect under the ubuntu ethic; it would imply that you felt that person did not exist.

An internal consultant who had been raised in a rural village became visibly upset after a meeting where nothing much had seemed to happen. When a project in which he'd played a key part came up for discussion, his role was not mentioned or acknowledged. Asked later why it had bothered him so much, he said, "You don't understand. When they spoke about the project, they did not say my name. They did not make me a person."

You could argue that we invoke each other's potential by our willingness to see the essence of the other person. It's that essence that I think we're all yearning for. That feeling of being seen. Just stop and imagine what others would feel like if we greeted each other this way all the time.

What if we stopped and let others know "I see you"? How do you think it would feel for you to be seen? How could you not be kind and speak kindly and want kindness for someone who sees you?

As Dr. Elizabeth Taylor, author of *Wisdom to Go*, stated, "It's a good thing to take the full measure of the man, woman, youth and child you meet along the way. It is noble to make the acknowledgement of the 'other' a valued everyday practice, and to exit each human exchange with the full satisfaction of knowing that you brought someone else into existence."

This is the essence of my compelling purpose, which centers on people being in deep conversation with each other, seeking to understand the other person. People sharing their brilliant and fabulous ideas and others being curious, listening intently, and welcoming—even actively asking for—conflicting ideas. Imagine a world where this exists.

I love technology and have been involved in that industry for several decades. I have been witness to what it has changed in our world. Yet I see more and more isolation of people as a result of current technical devices. Do you remember the experiment of the man who lived for one year in his home without ever leaving it? He was able to interact with others only via the Internet. He obtained every single thing he needed to live his life for an entire year via the Internet. I am finding that people currently lack the ability to be in meaningful and deep conversations with others. We are at our computers working solo, and we use our mobile devices to communicate with a restrictive 140 characters. We are never disconnected from the world, and yet we are never really connected with it either.

It's that connection that is missing. That heart-to-heart "I see you" connection. That validation that we do exist.

That's what I got in touch with in England. That's what started to shake me awake.

Soon after that workshop I attended an advanced workshop, and then I assisted at a third workshop. It was at that third workshop that my first bigger game became clear to me and I voiced it. "Create the largest women's conference in my county."

There. I said it. It was now out to the world. I had to do something, because one of the requirements of the bigger game is that you must speak your game. And . . . the synchronicity started happening. It got a life of its own. My hunger had to be fed. My compelling purpose had to be fulfilled.

The hunger and compelling purpose were a good enough reason to have me leave my comfort zones. Some of the comfort zone "best friends" I had to leave behind were using email instead of speaking on the phone or face to face; believing that "I have to do it all myself"; powering down by watching a lot of videos and TV; keeping constantly busy so I could say "I don't have the time for this game"; and staying in the dreaming/planning/obtaining knowledge/preparation phase instead of "just doing it."

Then came the gulp. The barrage of self-doubts became hard to dodge. My monkey mind began to squawk, causing me to feel unsettled, restless, confused, indecisive, and even uncontrollable at times. The negative voice in my head started to pull down on the reins, which caused it to become my most dominant voice. "Who am I to think I can do this?" "This conference is way too big for me to do." "I've never planned more than a dinner party for six . . . how can I plan something this size?" "I can't." "I don't have the expertise . . . money . . . connections . . . (fill in the blank)." "Blah, blah, blah." I was feeling that "GULP-y" place.

I needed to make the investment of time, money, and mental energy to learn how to do the things I didn't know how to do. After all, if you already know how to do it, it's not a Bigger Game. I learned how to fundraise and how to market a conference.

The best part is that I learned I didn't have to do this alone. I found co-players and allies and it became easier with others' help. They loved it because they were able to do what they loved doing. It was the best use of each of them. The great part about it was that there was a group of women who also wanted to do this; they had the answer to their "why" but just didn't know "how." We figured out "how" together.

It took us more than six months to make this vision a reality. During this time I was also running my full-time business and I needed to sustain myself by taking good care of myself, maintaining some balance in my life, getting enough rest, eating well, exercising, and "retreating" when I needed to into a good book, a visit to a museum, or a nature hike.

But as I said in my description of the Sustainability game piece, the game itself sustained me *and* itself! (Spoiler alert: we offered a second annual conference based on the success of the first.)

We spent time *assessing* along the way. We constantly asked ourselves, "What's working?" "What's not working?" We assessed our flyers, brochures, exhibitors, speakers, conference logistics, schedule—we even assessed our committee members to ensure we had the right skill sets.

Lastly, we kept taking bold action in what we did. "Let's ask for $20,000 instead of $10,000!" "Let's ask this company for a donation!" "Let's ask this person to (fill in the blank)."

The result? The first annual "Women Seeing Beyond Today" conference was held in South San Francisco, California. More than 250 women from different socioeconomic and ethnic backgrounds came together for the day to be in conversation with each other, to be inspired, and to know they could inspire others. Women who were validating each other. Women who knew they made a difference. They participated in and learned from twenty-four different workshops covering financial well-being, career planning, spirituality, personal growth, and creativity.

At the end of the day, as I sat in the conference hall and reflected on the day and how I got to this exact moment, I felt an amazing feeling of accomplishment. I truly felt that these women were in deep conversation with each other.

Another Bigger Game was now in the world.

The world is waiting for yours.

"We ask ourselves, who am I to be brilliant, gorgeous, talented, and fabulous? Actually, who are you NOT to be?"

This book will show you one way.

OTHER WOMEN'S BIGGER GAMES

To give you still more hope and courage and guts to play your next Bigger Game, I've included excerpts from interviews I had with seven gutsy women who have each played a Bigger Game. I pulled these seven from among transcripts of the thirty-four women I interviewed as I researched this book. I will admit my selection process was not a scientific one, but more an inspirational one. Some of the women I've known for a while.

Others inspired me when I first met or heard them, and I knew I wanted to get to know them better and hear their stories. All of the women I asked agreed to be interviewed for possible inclusion into this book.

I chose these seven humble women based on the diversity of the work that they do. I wanted to be sure to provide you, my reader, with varied sources of inspiration. These women represent diverse careers in agriculture, government, business, nonprofits, and entrepreneurship. I selected them because they have had a huge impact on the work they are doing and in their worlds. They are doing work that is "bigger" than they are, something they were called to do; yet when they first started, none of them knew "how." Each in her own right is an example of a servant leader. They did not have a clear sense of direction when they selected their Bigger Game and are at a place in their lives they never imagined they would be. They are at a place that is bigger than their biggest dreams.

None of these women knew about The Bigger Game model. But I knew that even though this model did not prompt their work, their work embraced the nine Bigger Game model game pieces. Each one, to a woman, could say, "Yes, this model was my thought process, even though I didn't have the model to follow along my journey." For instance, one of the women said, "I didn't call it my Compelling Purpose, I called it my career goal. It was just as big." Each was unknowingly living the pieces of the model.

If there are women out there who are living the model without knowing it, just think how you are able to make more changes in your life because now you have a tool, a map, a model. You are now able to look at your life with intention and choose the next best step on the game board. You are literally "ahead of the game" by having this model to help you fit your pieces together to move yourself toward achieving something new.

Over the next seven chapters, I'll tell you about the women's individual lives, their stories, so you can get to know each of them. You'll see how their lives fit into the Hunger, Compelling Purpose, Comfort Zones, GULP, and Bold Action game pieces of The Bigger Game model.

After the individual stories, there is one chapter each for the four generic model game pieces of Investment, Allies, Sustainability, and

Assess. These four chapters take a deeper look at what these women had to invest in to make their dreams, visions, and games real.

As you read these chapters, see if what these women experienced mirrors things that are, or have been, the same in your life. Maybe a comfort zone was no longer serving you and you knew it was time to leave; or perhaps you were just so exhausted you hit the proverbial wall and made the decision that *not* taking care of you had to stop. Or maybe, just maybe, the original plans you made had to change and you had to let go of something major when you took a hard look and assessed that it was best to just move on.

Or all of these.

All I ask is that you try to see yourself in each of these stories. Look for the similarities and not the differences. This perspective will help you in many areas of your life. As I stated early on, one of my goals for writing this book is to inspire you, the reader. Inspiration awakens us to new possibilities and transforms the way we perceive our own capabilities. In reading these stories and seeing how they align with The Bigger Game model, I believe you will see elements of your own journey and begin to say to yourself, "If they can do it, I can do it too."

I want you to see the possibilities and the solutions and, most importantly, your part in them.

I want you to become your own hero.

Chapter 3

....

DRU RIVERS, CO-OWNER OF FULL BELLY FARMS

....

Bigger Game: No Chemical Farming

Dru Rivers is the co-owner of Full Belly Farms, a four hundred-acre organic farm developed in 1984 in northwest Yolo County, California. She believes in farming as a way of life, and a way of providing good food for people and connecting with the land.

Dru grew up in a very rural area in Vermont, but her family were not farmers. They lived on a farm, but the land was leased to a farmer who lived locally. Even though she did not grow up in a farming family, she had parents who were enthusiastic gardeners with a big vegetable garden.

The love of produce came at a very early age for Dru. She vividly remembers picking corn and hearing her dad say they had to run in the house and put it in the pot to eat it right then. That is a vivid memory for her, and growing good food has always been a big part of her life.

Back in 1984, Dru and her husband were interested in organic agriculture and farming in general as a way to support themselves. They believed in the rural way of life, and they understood that small communities are interconnected and can work together to make rural life healthy and strong. Dru's big goal is to provide folks with not only good organic food, but also education about farming. Full Belly Farms hosts many field trips, craft visits, and other forms of education for new farmers, children, educators, and anyone else who's interested in organic farming.

HUNGER

When I asked Dru if her hunger came from the space of "No, not that," "Yes, more of that," or "Something is missing," she quickly answered, "As I look at my Bigger Game, I clearly see that my game has come from 'No, not that.' The 'No, not that' for me is clearly saying no to chemical agriculture.

"I went to the University of California at Davis as an undergraduate student. A lot of what I was learning was chemically oriented—how to use chemicals, from what we put into the soil to prepare it, to how we use chemicals in the actual growing of crops. The use of this large amount of chemicals to grow the food we eat did not resonate with me at all. Food is such a pure element to me that putting things on it seemed really wrong. That was one thing that I clearly remember in my college days and saying I didn't really want to buy into that picture.

"I think for me a hunger was also about disappearing farms. I grew up in Vermont in a really rural, strong, small community. I really felt a need to keep this rural way of life in my life and in my family. It seemed to me that one of the reasons that our sense of togetherness is breaking down is the lack of farms. There are scary statistics about the number of farms that are going out of business every day and are being gobbled up by more big corporate farms. Even aside from that, I really felt that we needed to feel revived again, and part of that revival is a strong farm economy. I believe that part of that strong farm economy comes from selling things locally and having connections with the consumers.

"This myriad of things makes a farm healthy, and I really wanted this.

> "Our deep respect for the land and its harvest is the legacy of generations of farmers who put food on our tables, preserved our landscape, and inspired us with a powerful work ethic."
>
> —JAMES H. DOUGLAS, JR.

I had a hunger for making this happen. When we started out, I saw that so many other people were hungry for what we were doing in so many ways; I just knew this was my bigger game. People were hungry not just for good food, but also for this connection with the land.

"People want to know where their food is from. They want to know that there are still healthy farms. They want to have this connection with us and with the land that grows the food that sustains them.

"When we go to the farmers markets we always joke around that we are selling more than just produce. Sometimes we feel like therapists at the market because people just love to talk about the farm life and what is going on. They want to learn and they are hungry to be a part of their own food, even if it is just knowing a little bit more of where it came from and how it was grown.

"In our Community Supported Agriculture (CSA) group, we do box delivery. We have over eight hundred families a week that get this CSA box. It has a newsletter we write every week about what is currently going on at the farm. In surveys we have done, people have said that they like the newsletter almost as much as the produce. It is that important to them, and some would still get it if it was just the newsletter.

"Seeing that need for people to understand where their produce comes from and have that connection with the farmers and then being able to fulfill that need, that feeds my 'more of that' hunger."

COMPELLING PURPOSE

"On an everyday basis, I love to eat and I love to cook and I love that connection. We have four kids, so for me there was, on a selfish level, a compulsion to provide good food for my family. And it was definitely a bigger picture for me too. I have always been compelled to teach people about whole, healthy food and eating well. Teaching them about food that is good for them is really important to me.

"Wanting to feed my family and others healthy foods is my compelling purpose. On a bigger picture, I work a lot with nonprofits. I was a director of a nonprofit that was called the Ecological Farming Association based out of Watsonville, California. We do a lot of educating farmers and consumers about agriculture and eating healthy. We teach people how to grow things organically. That is the bigger picture and fits in with my compelling purpose."

COMFORT ZONES

"Using the phrase 'comfort zone' is kind of funny. I often feel that the work that we are in is hard but also pretty comforting. The work I do is more about providing people with their own comfort zones. That comfort zone is healthy, good food.

"It is a political statement when we talk about farming organically. There is still a lot of opposition to it. People have strong feelings about it, so being confident and able to speak with clarity about the issues is important. I never liked being in the public eye, so leaving a comfort zone for me was learning to be more comfortable in sharing my message on a higher level with a larger audience. Learning how to best frame my message, know my audience, and then deliver it to a large number of people was having to leave my comfort zone.

> "I'm glad I don't have to make a living farming. Too much hard work. Too many variables you don't have control over, like, is it going to rain? All I can say is, god bless the real farmers out there."
>
> —FUZZY ZOELLER

"Our farm was featured in *National Geographic* in 1995 and that interview and all the attention that derived was really difficult for me, because I am not a public person. Farming appeals to me partly because of its solitude. We are very far away from a populated area. Being a public figure was very hard for me and that comfort zone of being a solitary person was one that I had to leave, as our farm is very active. There are always tours, and people are always calling for opinions and interviews. Being a public face for a movement, now that was hard."

GULP

"Just buying a hundred acres of land was a big gulp. I was only twenty-five and I had to have some farm experience to make this work. But, in reality, I didn't know what I was doing. We put a deposit on this place and suddenly I was supposed to know how to be a farmer.

"This was probably my biggest gulp. Suddenly, I had to keep down those doubts, those times that I kept saying, 'Who am I to think I know how to farm?' It was a very elaborate learning process until I stopped feeling this particular GULP and finally knew, in my heart of hearts, that I was a farmer.

"There were also gulps on the business side of farming. I had never kept financial books before. I was young. I had a job before buying the farm and was managing one of the farms at the University of California at Davis. There were no economics or financials that I had to be working with. I was just hired to help do the tractor work. So I really didn't know anything about farm economics or bookkeeping. Yeah, that was a big gulp.

"I feel like I still don't know some things about farming. So the gulp continues."

BOLD ACTION

"I have a great little story that explains what bold action means to me. This is perfect for me. My husband and I have the same saying when we need to take bold actions. What we say is, 'We'll just get the cow.'

"A while back, I really wanted a milking cow, so that we could have fresh milk. I never had a cow and had no idea how to handle them, but I wanted fresh milk really bad. We just went out and bought a cow without knowing anything about them. We got the cow and then we figured it all out after that. We figured how to milk and what to do with the milk. But if we never got the cow, we would never

> "In fact, because of their connection to the land, farmers do more to protect and preserve our environment than almost anyone else. They are some of the best environmentalists around."
>
> —IKE SKELTON

know what it was like. We bought a cow and now, sixteen years later, we have five cows.

"I feel like this is our motto. You just have to do it and you just have to try something. So some of our bold actions were buying the land, a little bit of going against the grain of what our families thought. My mom was hoping that I would be a botanist, not a farmer, so going against a little bit of what everyone thought made sense for our life. Basically, it's all about taking the bull by the horns and saying, 'Ok, I will try this and we will see how it goes.' It has worked about 90 percent of the time.

"My advice to others who are thinking about making a big move, but feel as if they just don't know how, is 'Just get the cow.'"

ASK YOURSELF . . .

- Dru believed in farming and the rural way of life. She wanted to keep the feeling of a rural community alive in her family. What is it that you want to keep alive in your life?

- When Dru thought about buying the land, she thought, "Who am I to think I know how to farm?" The thing is, she didn't know much about farming, but learned along the way. What is it that you say to yourself that may stop you from playing your bigger game? When are some times in the past that you said this type of thing to yourself, but went ahead and did it anyway?

- Dru talked about her bold action being that they "Just got the cow." What's the "cow" you need to get for your next bold action?

Chapter 4

·················

LIBBY TRAUBMAN, COFOUNDER OF THE JEWISH-PALESTINIAN LIVING ROOM DIALOGUE GROUPS

·················

Bigger Game: Find the Common Ground

Libby is the cofounder of the Jewish-Palestinian Living Room Dialogue Groups and a former trustee with the Foundation for Global Community. More than twenty-three years ago, Libby and her husband Len cofounded the Jewish-Palestinian Living Room Dialogue Group, in which people meet up in each other's living rooms in the San Francisco area. These men and women include Muslims, Christians, and Jews in face-to-face relationship building.

This initiative was inspired by Libby's work with the Foundation for Global Community, which served education and spiritual progress for many decades. The Foundation was a nonprofit educational community that responded to the needs of the times with creative initiatives aimed at bringing people into harmony with each other and with the planet. Its basic principle is that all of life and people are interrelated, interconnected, and totally interdependent—all truly one.

The Foundation continued for sixty years, a long time. With roots going back to the 1920s, the community evolved in name and form, depending on the needs of the times, for the good of all.

This unitive principle keeps inspiring Libby and Len to look at the big picture and to always consider, beyond their own interests, the greater global community. They believe the acts of each person can make a difference—and sometimes have a huge impact. The knowledge that every little choice matters continues to undergird and power their lives. As Libby says, "If you can't have fun building a better world, you're not yet doing it quite right."

Libby was part of that globally minded community that rejected violence and in 1982 birthed the successful movement Beyond War: A New Way of Thinking. This put her in an arena where she met a lot of different people from every continent. In 1991, Palestinian and Israeli citizen-leaders asked Beyond War to take them to California to meet face to face in depth. It was illegal for them to meet in the Holy Land.

"We thought it was a very interesting request because we didn't know anything about the conflict," said Len. "I'm Jewish, and at that time, I'd never met a Palestinian, except in my pediatric dental practice. Because of what we learned through the Foundation, our way of thinking, and the position we were in, we felt we could make something like this happen. We just said, 'Okay, let's see what we can do.'"

They requested help from friends at Stanford University's Center for Conflict and Negotiation, who were very excited to be a part of this potential healing. For three years, Libby and her husband worked together with others to find the right people, raise money, and make this conference happen.

They brought top-quality people to be in the conversation. At the conference, they signed a document, the first of its kind, called "Framework for a Public Peace Process." At the end of the working week, Len and Libby followed the participants back

> "If ever there comes a time when the women of the world come together purely and simply for the benefit of humankind, it will be a force such as the world has never known."
>
> —MATTHEW ARNOLD

to the Jerusalem area to help them gel as a team. They helped get the framework in the hands of Arafat, the Knesset, and other citizen-leaders. They really tried to get Jews and Palestinians to pair up and appear on TV and radio to get this document into the public's awareness.

That was a huge learning process for them. "We had never really studied or participated in anything like this, but after the three years of preparation, being at the conference with these people, and seeing this document emerge, we just said we can't stop now. We are invested."

So they asked themselves how they could continue this process of engagement and get more people to participate in this real-life experience. The answer to that question was the Dialogue's birth in their California living room. They just started inviting people they knew and others they didn't know by asking if they would be interested in meeting in a living room setting to talk to a Jew or a Palestinian. Some said they would love to, while others were not the least bit interested.

After a few months, there was a core team of that first San Mateo dialogue group: about fifteen brave and courageous people. It just kept growing—that original dialogue group is preparing for its 281st meeting. The offshoot, San Francisco Dialogue Group, which they also facilitate, will soon celebrate eighteen years and 199 meetings. Says Libby: "We have been meeting for over twenty-three years and have spun off many other dialogue groups. There have been over sixty across North America, beyond counting now."

They also go to college campuses and high schools, taking dialogue participants as exemplars to tell their stories. "We present the dialogue experience to the students because we know that there are a lot of different groups of people involved in conflict. And we feel that our personal narrative-sharing approach, based on the experience that an 'enemy is one whose story we have not heard,' is the way to begin." Libby models what it means to listen with compassion and to be interested in perspectives other than one's own. She teaches them how to really take in the "other" and drop one's own assumptions and previous beliefs in the moment—intending for participants to take on whole new ways of thinking, something that they can take home and consider to expand their frames of reference and learn to become much more inclusive.

"It is a process, and it has to be sustained. You can't just meet once and expect things to change. It is really an ongoing training to continue to learn, open up more, and then spread by giving other people this same experiential opportunity."

They still hold these meetings in each other's living rooms. That's part of the experience: having a Jewish person go into a Palestinian home and a Palestinian go into a Jewish home. Doing this, the visitor gets a feeling for what has meaning for the other family, what their culture is like, what they surround themselves with, and also how much they have in common. "Everyone has beauty in symbols," Libby says. "They love food, they take care of their children, you see the family pictures, and you begin to understand the sameness is much greater than the differences.

"As far as we know, it is the oldest sustained dialogue of its kind that has ever happened. They always start with what's personal. Groups who start with the personal and tell stories and learn what things mean to another person [are building] trust. When you can build trust with people and you see them as humans and as equals, then you are much better able to look at the political issues and be more open to solutions that you would have never given consent to otherwise. So you can really see people shift dramatically.

"We have had both Arabs and Jews come into the group and say, 'I have never met or sat personally with the other.' Sometimes they are shaking and they are very fearful. But when they meet each other, they just can't believe that they could develop a friendship."

Libby and Len continue to bring new friends together.

HUNGER

"For me, my hunger was brought about by knowing that something was missing. And what has been missing in many situations where it focuses on the Jewish-Palestinian relationship is the quality of listening. I think what we realized is simply that people are not listening to each other. They do not listen to their kids. They do not listen to their neighbors. And, they do not listen to the signs of the time and the warnings about what we are doing to the planet. We are not listening to what the environment is telling us. We are so busy trying to keep things going that we are not seeing the negative effect we are having in our keeping it going, on our planet and in our relationships.

"I feel like the quality of listening has been terrible, and there are a lot of people that are left out and not heard. When people are not heard and feel dismissed, they get very angry and frustrated and a little bit crazy. So we began these dialogues because the Palestinians and the Israelis were not able to listen to each other.

"The more we have gone to the college campuses and into the dialogue model with college students, the more we can see the frustrations the students experience when they have demonstrations. They feel no one is listening to the other and they are just trying to see who can out-scream and out-talk the other. I think what we have seen as missing is the public peace process and the quality of listening."

COMPELLING PURPOSE

Libby's compelling purpose continues to be the philosophy she lives by. She thinks her compelling purpose for this work is knowing, learning, and experiencing that we are all one. "If your end of the lifeboat has a hole in it, then my end does, too, and we are all in this together. I know there is not going to be an easy fix unless we are all part of the solution. I think that's what drives me and then what keeps me going."

Libby feels lucky that she has her husband as a partner who is totally committed to this. "We do it shoulder to shoulder because there are times that it can get exhausting or discouraging. One of the things that we agreed to is that we would not let the day's news pull us down. It is easy to look at the headlines and give up. We know that there are hurdles and ups and downs and good news and bad news. We try to make something work and just try to sustain the positive outcomes. There have been some disappointments, but there have also been some incredible stories and behind-the-scenes hopeful things that have happened that just keep us going. We have just agreed together that as long as we are healthy, this is what we are invested in. And we want to do the best we can for as long as we can."

COMFORT ZONES

"We had to leave a lot of comfort zones to make this happen. We had to travel to places we had not been. We went to the Soviet Union in 1984; Armenia and Azerbaijan; Palestine and Israel; and more recently Nigeria to bring together two hundred brave Muslims and Christians. We had to meet new kinds of people we had never engaged with before. We overcame doubts, fears, and the stereotypes we had been taught about 'others' foreign to us in our first four decades of life.

"I had to transcend my assumptions from growing up in Indiana— no small task. These were perceptions I was not conscious of, but once you begin to work intimately with a group of people, you begin to understand the things that you realize have colored your own thinking. We had to overcome stereotypes and a fear of traveling into lands that we were told were very dangerous."

> "An enemy is one whose story we have not heard."
>
> —MS. GENE KNUDSEN HOFFMAN

Public speaking is one of the greatest fears of most people who begin to play a bigger game. A Bigger Game Player is one who speaks to advance their game in the world and find allies. Says Libby: "One of my biggest fears is public speaking. I have never felt comfortable with public speaking, nor felt that I could do a good job speaking. I have had to do a lot of public presentations and have really pushed myself to do something that I never thought I would do. I have gotten more comfortable with it."

GULP

"I think one of the biggest gulps was feeling like I didn't know enough about the whole historical context. In the beginning, when we started the group, I didn't know that I didn't know. When I started hearing the different narratives and the people talking about their experience during the historical changes that have happened in Israel, I started thinking I did not know anything and feeling that I could not be much help here. So I had to do a lot of researching and reading and overcoming the doubts that I wasn't really the person that should be doing this.

"The other thing that was 'GULP-y' for me was the realization that I really did not need to have all the facts. I had to be more about the practice of dialogue and how that works. I think the gulp was that it was such a new arena for me and that I had not done anything like this before. I just had to overcome self-doubt.

"It seemed that my intention was good and my motivation was good. I was really for both peoples equally. I had to learn that it was okay if I learned along the way, and it was okay if I didn't have all the answers. We were still at a position where we could bring the people together, and that was the bottom line."

BOLD ACTION

"One of the first bold actions I took in the beginning was to cold-call people knowing that we wanted to start a dialogue group. One of the bravest actions for me was to find a Palestinian couple to agree to come to a dialogue meeting. Well, they didn't come. I was in conversations with them for months, when I finally said, 'I am not going to stop telling you about the meetings and asking you to participate until you either show up or you tell me to stop calling you.' After about six months, this Palestinian couple came with two other Palestinian couples. They formed our core group and helped to bring in other Palestinian families. For me, that was bold and gutsy because it was not something I was comfortable with. I had to push and insist in a nice way and tell them how much we needed them to participate.

"Being interviewed on panels, radio, and TV has been a bold action for me personally. It is way out of my comfort zone. I feel like most everything I do is a bold action, compared to my safe youth in Indiana. It has all been so challenging and new. It has been taking another step and another step and this bigger game just kind of pushes us along.

"We've had politicians like Israeli Yossi Beilin and Leah Rabin in the living room. We contacted Nabil Sha'ath, one of Arafat's right-hand men and still in the Palestinian political arena. We heard that he was going to be in our area speaking, and asked if he would come to our house to attend a dialogue meeting. 'Yes,' he said emphatically. The next thing we knew, Secret Service had sniffing dogs throughout our house and yard. The night he arrived, it was in a big motorcade and police posted around the house. So bold actions, yes. We are always working in very conflictual arenas.

"Yet, no less bold was our step together into filmmaking. I realized that people need and deserve stories of human successes, not just the failures seen on traditional news broadcasts. So since 2007, we've produced six how-to, inspirational films to show others what successful face-to-face communication looks like, and how possible it is. They include *Dialogue at Washington High* and *Twenty Years of Palestinian-Jewish Living Room Dialogue.*

"Requests for the films have come from citizens in over 2,500 institutions in 2,600 cities in ninety-two nations on every continent. We've gifted over fifteen thousand DVDs to these bridge builders, as people increasingly realize that nothing replaces heart-to-heart relationships—not borders, not treaties.

"The US State Department has distributed the films, and the Dialogue Group's model is additionally serving new African peace builders in Côte d'Ivoire, [Democratic Republic of] Congo, and northern Nigeria, plus so many others on all the continents.

> "One of the most sincere forms of respect is actually listening to what another has to say."
>
> —BRYANT H. MCGILL

"I have this quote on my desk that says 'Well-behaved women rarely make history.' I have interpreted this to mean that a quiet woman or a shy or withdrawn woman rarely makes history. It's not like I am trying to *make* history, but I am trying to *help* history. I feel like my participation in creating these opportunities to dialogue about differences has enriched my life to the point that it has helped me see the whole of myself. It has helped me to become a more compassionate person, a better listener, and to have more nerve to stand up for what I think is important.

"My advice for those who look around and see that something is missing is to just create a space for people to feel free to talk. Be curious and just let them talk. Your part is to listen very carefully to what they are saying and seek to understand. Listening can work magic."

ASK YOURSELF...

- For the sake of her game, Libby, as well as her husband, had to let go of the traditional leisurely retirement belief. "We have given up one lifestyle for this one, with absolutely no regret. It has been fabulous. And it's fun." What are beliefs that you must let go of for the sake of your game?

- Of the three lenses to look through and determine what we are hungry for ("No, not that," "More of that," or "What's missing?"), Libby was very clear that for her it was "What's missing?" She knew that what had been missing in many situations was the quality of listening to understand. She felt "there are a lot of people that are left out and not heard. When people are not heard and feel dismissed, they get very angry and frustrated and a little bit crazy." When you think of your hunger through those three lenses, what is it that "must be" in your world? What is it that causes people, and even you, to get "a little bit crazy"?

- Libby's game began because she was curious and willing to open up her living room to find her answers. What are you curious about? What might you open up your living room to conversation about in order to get answers to your questions? Watch out! You may be inviting a bigger game, as well as game changers, into your living room!

Chapter 5

·················

COURTNEY RUBY, FORMER CITY AUDITOR OF OAKLAND, CALIFORNIA

·················

Bigger Game: To Bring Integrity and Ethics into Local Politics

Courtney Ruby is very clear about her philosophy in life. She feels that in this journey of life we either deal with our fears or they deal with us. It's not in our time; it's in God's time. She firmly believes that anything is possible with a strong, enduring faith.

Courtney grew up in Ohio and attended American University, where she graduated with a degree in accounting. She never envisioned getting into politics. Her professor guided her into the accounting field, as she was so adept at it. Accounting became her passion and, following her heart, she got into this arena. She loved accounting and she loved Washington, DC. It all just came together for her.

Courtney was fortunate to work for one of the top women Democrats, Governor Ann Richards of Texas, and in national politics prior to her run for Oakland City Auditor. She was in her second year at Deloitte & Touche when Bill Clinton was out on the campaign trail. She was enamored with this charismatic leader who could light up the youth and engage them in a dynamic way so that they felt anything was possible. "Anything is possible" is a theme in Courtney's life, and she believed this attracted her to Clinton's philosophy.

Although she started her career as a CPA, she found it hard to both be a public accountant and make a difference in the way she felt she was capable. While at Deloitte & Touche, she took a two-week vacation to take a crash course in campaign management. It was at this time she started to feel like there was a bigger game out there for her. She started to feel that there was more for her.

> "My life is my message."
>
> —GANDHI

From that two-week intensive campaign management course at her alma mater, she went on to become one of the regional finance directors with Governor Ann Richards's 1994 reelection campaign. She continued on this path by becoming the deputy chief financial officer for the Democratic National Convention (DNC) in 1996. Her feet were planted in two worlds: public accounting and politics.

For Courtney, it was interesting that these worlds kept intersecting, because one does not envision public accounting and politics together. Yet that is who she is. There is one part of Courtney that wants things to line up and make sense, and another part that demands integrity and ethics be part of the equation; ultimately, the combination led Courtney to seek the position of city auditor. "Numbers don't lie, people do. We are all accountable for our actions. As the elected watchdog, I hold people accountable to correct errors and improve systems when I find government has failed to operate with integrity."

Courtney's idealism was challenged when she became very disillusioned by the Bill Clinton and Monica Lewinsky situation and the fallout that ensued. With all her idealism, she found it difficult to understand what was going on with the Clinton presidency, the DNC, and the nation during a time when everything she touched was under a subpoena.

This was an intense time for Courtney. Since she was contemplating becoming a member of the clergy at this time, she moved to the West coast to pursue ministry. She has always been very spiritual. It is what grounds her. It is what guides her. After working in a ministry for about five months, it became very clear to her that politics was to be her ministry. She realized she is here to make a difference for all people—not just a certain group of people who belong to a certain faith.

In 1999, her journey became getting over her fear of being in the forefront. She moved to Oakland, and in 2006 she ran for office. For seven years before taking that action, she worked on slaying her demons, knowing that one day she would be called to step out. The fear she felt was about taking this political role. She is very intuitive and had known for a long time that her bigger game was not about her being behind the scenes. She finally got to a place where she felt okay to be in the public eye. She was confident it was her time now.

It is interesting that as Courtney tells it, it was not in her time; it was really in God's time, because her mother had just passed away when she decided to run for office. She was in a very painful personal place and yet she knew this was the office she was to run for. "I knew it was my time, but I would not have laid things out like that. Certainly in the campaign, I felt that I was really numb, going in and out of grief and being present in this really intense way."

When she took the oath of office, her new department was going through significant challenges. Her predecessor experienced issues of sexual harassment and a hostile work environment that were published in the media. When Courtney took over, she only had a few staff members remaining from the previous administration and staff members were literally taping their desks back together. She cleaned house and committed to creating a model performance-audit organization that would return in-depth and meaningful results to the citizens of Oakland. In her six years in office, Courtney has been able to expose significant cultural and ethical issues that have held the city back for years. She has fought to shine a light on what is not working and demand better for the citizens of Oakland and in doing so has garnered significant support from the citizens of Oakland. She was first elected with over 65 percent of the vote, and was then reelected with almost 67 percent of the vote.

It's been an incredible journey for Courtney.

HUNGER

"My hunger goes back to the place where anything is possible. When I look at what is driving us forward as a country, or even as an organization, I very much believe that our choices define our reality and how we live our lives. You can look at the glass half empty or half full. This is the way I have lived my life in the midst of a really challenging story with trauma, losses, and much more.

"I believe this time is an incredible opportunity. People need to be inspired. They need to know they can make a difference. They need to know that others care. For me personally, it is where I get to the edge and I have to jump off. It's like there is something there; that I can't turn back. I know I am here to do more, be more, and create more.

"What drives me is the life I am creating. Because I believe that I am here to serve others, I have a responsibility. At the end of the day, it can't be about me, because if it's about me, then I am pretty lifeless. This doesn't work for me.

"If it is about serving others, making a difference, making a better world, then I am engaged. There has been a lot of fear in my journey—fear about 'Is this mine to do? Am I the one? Do I trust that I know?' The part of feeding my hunger is I know I am here to make a big difference, and the only thing that keeps me from making a big difference is my fear.

"If I truly believe I am a vehicle of change, then I have got to move out of my own way, and I have to step into the battles as they present themselves."

COMPELLING PURPOSE

"My compelling purpose goes back to making a difference and making the world a better place. We have this amazing city called Oakland that should be one of the jewels of cities. We have this history and this narrative about corruption and dysfunction and lack of integrity and ethics and culture, and it is like . . . Really? We go back to choice. Living in Oakland, we are making these choices to have our city look like this. If you look out, and believe we create what we put into the model, we have created this. We have created a city that struggles. We have created a violence issue. We have created a large citizenry that believes that they are disempowered. We have a dysfunctional government and we have a lot of issues about integrity and ethics in relation to culture.

"In this office, I see my work as being the truth teller. I have been the one who comes in and speaks truth to power. I have been the one to say that it is not okay.

"Within the first year I was here, I took on the former city administrator who was abusing power. I had to be the one to say that it is not okay.

"Everything comes down from the top. As with all leaders, the top models the behavior and needs to inspire. We have this amazing city and our workers have got to look up to someone and know that their work makes a difference and is moving the city forward.

"The citizens have to believe that somebody with ethics and integrity is driving the ship. So there is this level where, and this is so much of Oakland's story, it is okay if we don't play by the rules. And I say, 'No, it is not okay, because those choices that you are making are impacting everyone's lives.' Our businesses are leaving. Our schools are dysfunctional. I am here to call it, and what a wild ride that has been.

"People lined up and hoped I would fail. I have not and I will not. I believe that this city could be a model city for the US. I am here to help make that happen."

COMFORT ZONES

"I like change, so I cannot say that I am one who really thrives in a comfort zone. I am one who, if I get too comfortable, I am looking for where I go next in relation to my impact. I think as an elected official, for the first time, I am in a position that continuously challenges me. You have so many dimensions that you are operating on to impact change. Every day is different. So in that relationship, I feel I can move out of my comfort zones pretty quickly as my work demands it.

"It goes back to my hunger and compelling purpose. If I am here to make a difference and to serve and I stay in my comfort zone, then I am wasting who I am in that equation. I am willing to go anywhere that I can make the biggest difference.

"In 2003 and 2004, I went to Africa to serve children. That was probably the hardest and scariest thing I have ever done. I lived there by myself. I knew I needed to push myself further than I ever did before. That is why I am who I am. I am creating something greater than just for me. In Africa, for the first time in my life, I really got who I am and what I'm capable of, because it was so hard. It was the best year of my life and the hardest year of my life, but I surprised myself and I was proud of me.

I got what I was made of on a different level. I had taken risks before, but never like this. It was before I ran for political office and it was a very important part of my journey into where I am today."

GULP

"There always has to be a gulp. The gulp for me was to come on board and to really believe that people wanted a city auditor with integrity and ethics. It was a gulp to trust that through my actions the other elected leadership and the citizens would see this role as valuable and that I was the one bringing value.

"When I first stepped into office, they wanted business as usual. Initially, I didn't have support. I was going after the city administrator, and the city administrator and other officials' strategy was to discredit me.

> "I've learned that people will forget what you said, people will forget what you did, but people will never forget how you made them feel."
>
> —MAYA ANGELOU

"I found this fascinating because I am very spiritual. This is how I lead my life and I am willing to go it alone. It doesn't bother me because I am holding on to God. But it was hard coming in as a newly elected official and knowing out of the gate I have to execute perfectly, because this sets the tone for my administration—and will determine my ability to impact Oakland. How I execute and how I show up is who I am. Integrity and ethics are what I stand for and must be my guidepost every step of the way. I have to believe that I am going to do this and no one will scare me away from what I believe. I have to find the courage to tell them 'You are not going to block me from investigating this or that or auditing this or that.'

"I have learned that I need to lead from my inner knowingness. When I am looking out at people and wishing they were holding a higher ground or doing things differently, I have to trust that inner knowingness and move forward.

"Politics can be very cutthroat and very nasty. It is the part of politics that I dislike very, very much. In order to stand in my integrity and ethics through some situations, I remind myself that politics is my ministry. I feel the gulp many times and I trust I will continue to lead and that I will be the political leader that I am to be and not the political leaders others think I should be."

BOLD ACTION

"The first bold action I took in this job was taking on the city administrator right off the bat. And right now, I am auditing the city council—and they never thought that day would come. The council is not allowed to interfere in the administrative affairs. We have a new city administrator who I am very impressed with. She made it clear that she would not tolerate council interfering in administrative affairs in the city, which some council members had blatantly been doing for years. As the auditor, you cannot go in and audit the council if the administrator is not holding them accountable. It doesn't work. We are going in now and auditing the noninterference clause in the city charter.

"We audited the Fox Theater, renovated by one of the largest developers here. We went in and looked at that project and issued a report. I had to ask the council how a project could go from $30 million to $90 million. The council should be outraged, but no, because they have relationships with the developer, they were perfectly fine that the project's scope grew and it cost the city significantly more than originally budgeted. Somebody asked me about my political future when I did that. I was surprised. Am I here to do a job for the citizens of Oakland with integrity, or am I here to worry about my political future? Being objective and independent is my professional responsibility.

> "It is past time for women to take their rightful place, side by side with men, in the rooms where the fates of peoples, where their children's and grandchildren's fates, are decided."
>
> **—HILLARY CLINTON**

"There was a security contract for the City Hall Plaza up for bid. The staff recommended the first-rated contractor get the award, but the fifth-rated contractor is the one who has the contract and has had it for thirteen years. There was something wrong with this and I went down and sat in the committee hearings. I watched. They disregarded the staff recommendation and recommended that the contract go to the fifth-rated contractor.

"I called the city attorney and asked if they could do that. According to city charter they can. I then asked the question, 'How do we stop this?' If we don't stop this, the workers don't believe in you and you don't change the city. It so happened that some of the contractors had given campaign contributions to some of the council members during the RFP (Request for Proposal) process. This is not allowed. So even though campaign contributions is not my jurisdiction, I wrote a letter to the Public Ethics Commission and it went public that the firm, who ranked fifth and who the council was recommending receive the contract award, gave $1,800 in donations while competing for the contract, which is in violation of Oakland's campaign reform laws. National Public Radio covered it.

"I am serving the constituents and they need to know what is happening in their city. There was so much pressure against the city council for their actions, they awarded the contract to the number one staff recommendation. This was a big win. I walk across the plaza and the workers thank me because they want to work for a city that plays by the rules."

ASK YOURSELF . . .

- Spirituality is what grounds and guides Courtney. Always has and always will. She left ministry school when she realized she is here in this lifetime to make a difference for all people, not just a certain group of people who belong to a certain faith. What grounds you and guides your life?

- Courtney refers to "slaying her demons" prior to running for public office. She worked on preparing herself to be in the front of a room, to be capable of being in her position, to get over her fears. What dragons are you slaying in preparation for beginning and fully playing your bigger game?

- Throughout her story, Courtney is very clear that she knows she is here to make a difference as a leader in the world, and to make this difference she needs to determine what issues are holding her back and what work she needs to do. If you know you are here to make a difference, what are the top two or three issues holding you back? What work must you do to move these obstacles out of your way so you can move forward?

Chapter 6

....

SANDY HOFFMAN, FORMER CHIEF DIVERSITY OFFICER, CISCO SYSTEMS

....

Bigger Game: Transform Diversity and Inclusion for the Twenty-First Century

Sandy lives by the words of Eleanor Roosevelt: "If you approach each new person you meet in a spirit of adventure, you will find yourself endlessly fascinated by the new channels of thought and experience and personality that you encounter."

During the early part of Sandy's life, she found that she was doing things because other people, strong influencers in her life, guided her and helped her to make decisions. Yet Sandy always felt the pull of her own dreams and desires. So she stepped out of doing what others thought was best for her and began to follow what she knew was her path.

Early in her career at Apple Computer, she wanted to work under Steve Jobs' leadership and had the determination that no matter what, she was going to work within the Macintosh division, which Jobs oversaw at the time. She knew this was more than being a part of Apple; it was about working under one of the greatest leaders and innovators of our time. Through perseverance, she got there.

> "We cannot change what we are not aware of, and once we are aware, we cannot help but change."
>
> —SHERYL SANDBERG

She found she wanted more and was intrigued and fascinated by the differences, and yet similarities, cultures around the world had to offer. She wanted to experience many cultures and their daily events, so she sought roles that would allow her to travel internationally, stretch her to be uncomfortable, and open her mind to new possibilities.

Through this journey she realized, "It was no longer about me or my aspirations. It was something bigger that started to drive me and shape my career. It is funny that I found it late in life, but now I feel as if I am 'home' and it is time to start to actively participate, contribute, and help others find their voices and aspirations."

Sandy feels she has always been a late bloomer. But now, knowing where she is, the impact she can make, and the relationships she has developed, this all has enabled her to not only realize her own potential but also to help others realize theirs.

She is only the third Chief Diversity Officer (CDO) appointed at Cisco Systems, and came into this position with no human resources background, which is very nontraditional. Prior to becoming CDO, Sandy worked in global supply chain operations at Cisco, where she led their global manufacturing operations.

What moved her to get into the CDO role was her passion for building high-performing teams. Her global work provided her the opportunity to work with different cultures and perspectives and to find out what motivates people. "Every day you work with individuals around the world—assemblers, buyers, and executives. You have to balance the demands of the global pressures, variables within the process, and personal lives. How do you motivate people to want to come to work every single day, to feel they belong, are respected, heard, valued, and matter in a hierarchal structure where things move quickly?"

Sandy kept asking this question and knew she needed to find a way to tap into the potential of every person on the team in helping him or her to achieve their highest potential. To help her teams, she worked with a boutique outside consulting firm that was known for their innovation in inclusion and diversity (I&D). At the time she had no idea what I&D meant. She knew what she wanted to create but was not clear on how to make that happen. She was coached on the principles and behaviors of I&D, and she implemented models that ultimately transformed her leadership team. Given her past success and passion for this work, she was selected for a two-year assignment to set I&D strategy across the entire operations, process, and systems organization within Cisco.

Accepting this assignment was a difficult decision for Sandy, but knowing it was only a two-year commitment, she took the challenge. It did not take her two years to realize her passion. She knew there was a need and a desire to improve inclusion and diversity inside of Cisco, and she wanted to take it further. "It was either sit on the sidelines or jump in, join the game, and make a difference, something my father instilled in me in my early life. There are a few times in your life when everything aligns, and you are in a position to play a bigger role. I knew this was one of those times. There was a hunger and strong desire in me to do this." With the support of her mentors, colleagues, close business associates, and friends, she applied for and was accepted into the recently vacant CDO role for Cisco.

Sandy respects the traditional role of the diversity office but at the same time is trying to evolve it, disrupt it, and create something of a revolution. In doing this, there is a feeling of being a bit of a "lone wolf."

"I think that's where gutsy women and very powerful women cause some level of disruption without destruction. So you have to attach your want to disrupt to something larger than yourself. I want to respect the legacy and the history and learn from those who paved the way before me and create the change in the twenty-first century. You have to collide these elements of the past and future to create this new transformational thinking. That is what I am trying to do in the I&D office at Cisco."

Sandy is just the woman to do it.

HUNGER

"In my global supply chain operations role, I mostly went to the outskirts of a city where most of our contract manufacturing factories are. Here I got to see many different cultural norms. One can either learn to be color-blind to these places and the cultures, or you can embrace them and the beauty and differences they bring.

"Many times while visiting these sites, I was engaged in the processes, machine output, and yield, and not even aware of the people around me, who they were, their life experiences and what motivates them.

"As you get older and wiser, you see beyond the machines and process, and see that there are people operating these machines and executing the processes your team designed. Once you really see the people, you ask, 'How can you tap into the capabilities, knowledge, desires, and full potential of all these individuals?' When I felt that hunger, I started to look at all the opportunities available and what I could learn and pay it forward for others.

"I have seen some amazing things and experienced a lot in my life. Not just what you read on social media or see on television, but to truly experience it first hand. You have a choice of doing what is only asked of you or going beyond what is asked and looking at ways to transform the business and people's lives.

"When you get to work with such diverse teams, you can see the possibilities and the impact it can have on corporations and society as a whole. Cisco is a unique company because of its size and influence. It creates a platform and opportunity for you to influence change. So when you open your mind to it, all of a sudden you see the ability to impact sustainable change."

COMPELLING PURPOSE

"One of my strengths is to connect the unconnected and create opportunities and help others see and realize them. I have the opportunity to work with some incredible people in helping to shape the future for the next generation.

"We are witnessing many things taking shape that are going to make monumental transformations of our world as it exists today. With the speed of innovation, and moving through the knowledge era, we must rethink how we are leveraging the true potential of our human capital and knowledge that exists in all of us.

"We have to take all of our leadership practices from the twentieth century and look at them through a new lens, where the table stakes are higher. I am in a unique position, which I get to shape, design, and be a part of it. We all do.

"I do this not only because of my role, but also because of the position and platform that I have been given. This becomes my higher purpose. It is about the contributions and impact that it is making."

COMFORT ZONES

"I am not only an introvert, but I am also shy. The idea of public speaking would tie knots in my stomach, and I would avoid it at all cost. I learned how to reach out of my comfort zone and speak in front of a thousand people for the sake of my bigger game. I am able to do this by remembering that it is not me speaking, it is the one thousand people I am speaking for. That reminder makes it comfortable and safe for me to say, 'Yes! I need to go do this for the thousand people behind me. It's not about me.'

"Every day, I need to be able to break out of my comfort zones. I have a learning disability, as well. I can get ahead of myself too quickly when I speak. When people ask me to read things, it is terrifying to me, because I would stumble over words and be afraid of how others would perceive me. The number of events you are asked to participate in is very demanding in this role. I would love to stay behind the scenes, but the job requires me to be out in front leading at times."

GULP

"I always get that 'GULP-y' feeling when I have to take that one step and I don't know whether I'm going to free fall down or if there will be something or someone to catch me. I have been told to 'Go bold or go home.'

"Sometimes when you're at that edge, you need to pull it back a notch. We have all had that moment when we know we might have gone too far and wanted to pull back or have the ability to do it over. The one thing I have learned is to know enough about your audience and how far I can take them before I lose them or they are no longer interested.

"I am here not only to do this job but also to transform this job. I am

> "Do one thing every day that scares you."
> —ELEANOR ROOSEVELT

always 'GULP-ing.' I know that when I go back to what I believe, pushing that envelope, having people ask 'Huh?' and staying to learn more, this is when I know I am in the gulp and starting to have people listen and engage.

"If I go too far off, I have gone off the ledge. So I constantly gauge and educate myself on what the topics are. At times, I need to challenge myself not to fall into the 'me too' stage or engage in group thinking. When I go there, I find I stifle my ability to think big and dream big."

BOLD ACTION

"'Be bold or go home.' Being bold is about what you are going to do and what role you are going to play to make a better future. We all have a role to play. As world citizens, we all have a voice and it is important how we use it. The only question we need to ask ourselves is how big do you want to go? Do you want to do it on a professional level? Or do you want to do it on a personal level? Or both? How big do you want to go in creating? That is why we are all here.

"I question myself and reflect every week on what I have done. How big did I go? Nine times out of ten, I will always say I could have gone bigger. I get bogged down on the administration work or on going into my comfort zone or I simply question my ability.

"I look around at what people are doing in this world today and I start to be inspired by what I see and the changes they are making. What they are doing may not be for you. Only you can decide what is bold for you. Once you've decided and take action, then you have to hold yourself accountable. Your boss could hold you accountable, but at the end of the day it is really about how you are

> "I always did something I was a little not ready to do. I think that's how you grow. When there's that moment of 'Wow, I'm not really sure I can do this,' and you push through those moments, that's when you have a breakthrough."
>
> —MARISSA MAYER

going to feel when you walk away, and answer the question, 'Did I give it my all?'

"At the end of the day, you are the only one who knows what your performance was. I want to make sure that when I go out, I know that I gave it every single effort I could, and that I did not hold back. My advice to game changers is to be bold and adventurous. Inspire others to do the same."

ASK YOURSELF . . .

- Sandy talks about loving to connect the unconnected and create opportunities for others. This is a big part of finding allies. There are allies waiting out there to be a part of what you are creating. As she says, "I have the opportunity to work with some incredible people in helping to shape the future for the next generation." Who are the incredible people that will help you in shaping your bigger game?

- Sandy states that she is an introvert, shy, and also has a learning disability. Every day she must leave these comfort zones, no excuses, for the sake of making an impact. This doesn't sound very easy to me, an extrovert, and I imagine it is a very difficult thing to do. What are the parts of you, along with your beliefs and assumptions around those parts, that you must leave behind for the sake of your game?

- Be bold or go home. Per Sandy, "Being bold is about what you are going to do and what role you are going to play to make a better future. We all have a role to play. As world citizens, we all have a voice and it is important how we use it. The only question we all need to ask ourselves is how big do you want to go?" How big do *you* want to go?

Chapter 7

....

ANNE FIRTH MURRAY, FOUNDING PRESIDENT OF THE GLOBAL FUND FOR WOMEN

....

Bigger Game: Creating Justice in the World by Funding Women's Human Rights Initiatives

Activism is in Anne's blood. She is the founding president of the Global Fund for Women, which raises and gives away money to women's groups around the world, supporting women's human rights. She has authored two books *Paradigm Found: Leading and Managing for Positive Change* and *From Outrage to Courage: The Unjust and Unhealthy Situation of Women in Poorer Countries and What They Are Doing About It*. She teaches international women's health and human rights and love as a force for social justice at Stanford University. In the 1980s, she worked for the William and Flora Hewlett Foundation, where she directed population and environmental programs. In 2005, she was one of a thousand women jointly nominated for the Nobel Peace Prize.

In 1987, Anne founded the Global Fund for Women (GFW) for the purpose of raising money to fund women's groups working on female human rights issues around the world, particularly in resource-poor countries.

GFW believes that women are powerful catalysts for change and that strong women's organizations and movements can make transformative shifts in power that are crucial to women realizing their rights and

> "Women's rights are human rights."
>
> —HILLARY CLINTON

creating lasting solutions to the world's problems. By 2015, GFW had given away more than $125 million to about five thousand groups in 175 countries.

An example of a GFW grantee is a group of women in Korea who work with women at all levels of society to create a hotline and support center for battered women. The GFW grant was the first one they received when they began the organization. Another example is a network of African women based in East Africa working on women's legal rights, inheritance rights, and related issues for women.

Some of the organizations are local to a city or village; others are regional networks working on "human rights" as defined by these networks.

The overarching issues that GFW focuses on include ending gender-based violence, economic and political empowerment, and sexual and reproductive health and rights.

HUNGER

All three of the hunger lenses had an impact on Anne.

When we spoke of the "No, not that" lens, Anne focused on violence against women. That's a "No: this cannot happen." When she researched and studied what was happening in the world, she viewed gender violence as a key problem that had to be addressed. "I believe that we can work toward a world where injustice is not only made visible but addressed. There do not have to be people that are constantly poor and battered and beaten, and we can move to a different way."

When she reflected on the second lens, "More of that," the place where something is in place and is working, she saw that there were places where gender equality was improving ever so slightly, and she wanted more of that.

The third lens, "What's missing?" is where she saw this big black hole in the area of relating to each other. This is what she found to be missing in the world: that what we need is a new paradigm of relationships, a different way of relating to each other primarily across sexual differences.

Says Anne: "I've always been interested in the differences of men and women and the way women are treated in society. And 'what's missing' is a model or paradigm that allows us to be relating to each other in ways that are healthy and just and safe.

"This wasn't what necessarily drove me in the beginning when I started the organization, but as the organization began to develop I was driven, and I am now driven, by a desire to change the way we relate to each other.

"What's missing? I think what's missing is the sense that it is possible—across many countries, many people, many societies—to have a way of relating that is not hierarchical. We need a way of relating that is not either/or, win/lose, I'm up/you're down, I'm rich/you're poor. I believe that if we could change this way of relating and move away from the concept of something that is hierarchical and competitive toward something that is even-handed and collaborative and respectful, we would advance the rights of women and girls significantly.

"This desire for a paradigm shift in human relations is what drives me."

COMPELLING PURPOSE

Anne did not hesitate to say that making injustice visible is her compelling purpose.

"There was a personal drive that led me toward creating the Global Fund. I haven't had a bad life, but a lot of personal things happened to me early on that reminded me that life wasn't fair.

"My parents assumed that my brother would go to university. It was not assumed that I would go, although I did simply because I was so young and my parents thought it was a way to fill in the time before getting married. It was not 'You will go to a university and you will become a professional.' It was 'You are only sixteen. We don't want you out in the world just yet, so why don't you go to a university?'

"My brother had a life insurance policy taken out on him, and when I was about eight years old, I asked, 'Do I have one?' My mother said, 'Oh no, dear, you are going to get married and a man is going to look after you. You don't need a life insurance policy.' I remember thinking that

> "We all fight over what the label 'feminism' means but for me it's about empowerment. It's not about being more powerful than men; it's about having equal rights with protection, support, justice. It's about very basic things. It's not a badge like a fashion item."
>
> —ANNIE LENNOX

these situations were not fair. I had a clear sense that life was unfair merely because I was a girl and not a boy.

"For most of my life, if I pass somebody like a 'bag lady,' a woman who is a homeless person on the street, I often identify with that woman. I didn't grow up in a poor family; I didn't grow up in a wildly rich family either, but I thought, 'There but for the grace of God go I.' Perhaps that person made a choice, it seems the wrong one; and it scared me because I often thought how easily I could be that person."

Anne said something that a lot of the other women I interviewed and those that I work with have also said. When they were able to look at what they hungered to change in the world and what they believed their compelling purpose was, all these women felt that they "didn't have a choice." They felt driven to follow their paths.

As Anne said, "I was completely driven to make GFW work. This idea, this concept, struck me as such a good idea. It was a really good idea to raise money and give it away to women's groups who needed it. I had traveled the world and seen plenty of women's groups working for justice. I was knowledgeable about these issues, and I knew there was a niche that I could contribute to. There were small groups with no access to money, and I was in the philanthropic world where there was plenty of money. It just wasn't getting to them. I thought this was just plain silly. I looked at the situation and thought, 'This isn't logical.' So it made sense that once the idea got into my head of creating a public foundation, which is what the Global Fund is, I was driven to make it work. I can't think of another time in my life when I had such a compelling drive."

COMFORT ZONES

"A challenge to one of my comfort zones for me was leaving a regular salary. Once I got the idea of GFW in my head, I didn't have much choice about what direction I would take. When I started the Global Fund, there was no money. Because I was dedicated to the idea, I worked as a volunteer for the first two years for the Fund while I worked at a full-time job to cover my living expenses.

"After that time, I started working as salaried employee at GFW. I reduced my salary by thousands of dollars from my previous job, which itself was not very highly paid.

"At the time I was making this decision, there was another steady, good salaried job available. After some thought, I concluded that I was compelled to take on the Global Fund for Women rather than that job.

> "Throughout history, it has been the inaction of those who could have acted; the indifference of those who should have known better; the silence of the voice of justice when it mattered most that has made it possible for evil to triumph."
>
> **— HAILE SELASSIE**

"One might say it was a big risk for me to reduce my salary, but honestly, it didn't feel like a risk to me at the time."

GULP

"My book *Paradigm Found: Leading and Managing for Positive Change* is part memoir, part history, and part 'how to do it.' In the book, I talk about having done some public speaking prior to starting the Global Fund, but feeling nervous about speaking in front of big audiences. I knew that leading the Global Fund would involve being able to clearly and succinctly articulate what it was I was asking for. I had always been a little bit shy about getting up in front of groups of people. I kept asking myself 'Can I do this?' I was still a volunteer and I was deciding what I was going to do. I finally stopped asking myself that question when I made the decision that I was going to run the Global Fund. I thought the organization might actually take off, and if it did I would need to give lots of presentations and talk to large groups of people. I took a one-day workshop on how to make a speech. It really helped, and I have referred back to the workshop materials many times. I still feel a gulp when I am asked to speak, but not nearly as much as I used to."

BOLD ACTION

Anne was very humble when it came to our conversation around "bold action." Someone once asked her to write a chapter on women of courage taking risks because they thought she was one such woman. "Honestly, writing that chapter was hard for me to do because, frankly, I don't think that much of what I did was risk taking, even though a lot of other people thought it was.

> "The thing women have yet to learn is nobody gives you power. You just take it."
>
> —ROSEANNE BARR

"I guess one of the bold actions I took was that I jumped into running the GFW without an income. I guess that was bold action, but I didn't think I had much of a choice. I was quite driven to make this happen, so to me it wasn't really a bold action. It quite simply had to happen.

"People sometimes describe my attempt to be entirely honest and call it as I see it as a bold action. As I described what our work was really all about, I told people that if we are going to change the world, we needed to do it with love.

"Sometimes I feel that talking about the organization in terms of love is a bold action. I remember in one of our annual reports, I described what we were doing as love, and people were very surprised that I used that word.

"One time, someone called me an unrealistic idealist. I told them to look at the Global Fund for Women and know that it would not have become a reality if I had *not* been an unrealistic idealist. Many people had said that it couldn't happen. But it did and became something very real. It seems that being an unrealistic idealist may be necessary if one is to play a bigger game. Was it unrealistic to think that people would be good? Was it unrealistic to think that people would give money to help women? Was it unrealistic to think that men would open up their pockets and write checks and go out of their way to help us and to help women? Was it unrealistic to think that you could start from nothing and grow the organization into the millions of dollars? Was this unrealistic? Or idealistic? It was certainly idealistic."

Anne is truly an open and honest woman who challenges people's ways of thinking. In her book *From Outrage to Courage: The Unjust and Unhealthy Situation of Women in Poorer Countries and What They Are Doing About It*, she says that the issue of violence against women is one of the major human rights violations of our time. In the book, she documents other outrageous abrogations of women's rights. Some people have described her as bold for saying such things. Anne doesn't see it that way. "I don't think it is bold to say what's true. I think the bold aspect of a lot of this for me was to be willing to be what one might call an arch feminist. I speak up when I think something is outrageous and unjust."

Anne's advice to those who are stepping into their bigger games is that if you are feeling a compelling drive to go in a certain direction, go there. Listen to your heart.

ASK YOURSELF . . .

- One of Anne's driving forces in her life was that she knew, for her, life was unfair. There were differences between the way she was treated and the way her brother was treated. Where in your life do you notice life is unfair?

- Anne knew that a compelling principle in her life was justice. Noticing that life is unfair, she worked to make injustice visible. What do you want to see be different? What would you change if you had a magic wand?

- What three bold actions that make you gulp can you take in the next five days to pull you closer to getting in touch with your hunger and finding your compelling purpose?

Chapter 8

···············

SHARI SPENCER, MIXED MARTIAL ARTS ATHLETE MANAGER

···············

Bigger Game: Help Athletes Turn Their Competitive Success into Commercial Success

Shari was introduced to the sport of Mixed Martial Arts (MMA) through a friend who was treating MMA athletes holistically. "I didn't know anything about Mixed Martial Arts or even watch boxing before our conversation. But through him, I got to know the fighters and started caring about what happened to them." Shari also discovered a large gap in the fighters' representation—many were managed by their trainers or former fighters, largely because the revenue generated by MMA athletes, outside of a handful of elite fighters, was too low to attract the larger agencies to the sport.

Randy Couture, a coach on a reality show called *The Ultimate Fighter*, was one of the first fighters that Shari got to know. As he learned of her business background, over twenty years in corporate finance, including CFO of both public and private companies, she says, "He started to pick my brain and ask me for my advice on a few business opportunities he was looking into. At that time, he was still

> "If somebody offers you an amazing opportunity but you are not sure you can do it, say yes—then learn how to do it later!"
>
> —RICHARD BRANSON

actively fighting and training other fighters. But he was also approaching retirement and wanted to transition into several new businesses that he could lend his name and likeness to, and he was trying to figure out which ones made the most sense strategically. Initially, I was helping him here and there over dinner, but it quickly became apparent he needed someone who could dedicate much more time to evaluating options and setting up these businesses. So I recommended that he get somebody to help him figure out his business strategy and be a business advisor. I told him I would be happy to continue to help him, but given the time needed, I would have to start charging him. I never expected him to take me up on the offer, but he hired me on the spot."

Shari helped Randy set up a corporate structure and put business processes and procedures into place. She helped him decide what business offers would be profitable for him in the long run. "It gave me a great glimpse at a professional athlete approaching their retirement and the decisions they were faced with."

About a year later, she met Georges St-Pierre, a highly ranked fighter. In contrast to Randy, Georges was only in his mid-twenties and had not yet reached the prime of his career. He had actually won the welterweight title but then lost it in his very first title defense. He already had a manager, who was also a promoter, but he needed someone who could give more time and attention to a fighter of his high profile. Initially, Shari hesitated to become his manager; while she was able to utilize her business expertise in assisting Randy, she lacked previous experience managing an athlete. Yet after a bit of due diligence on what was involved, plus a genuine affection for Georges and a desire to help him, she finally agreed to work with him. Shortly thereafter, he was able to regain the title and remained the welterweight champion for the duration of their four-year working relationship.

> "There are many talented people who haven't fulfilled their dreams because they overthought it, or they were too cautious, and were unwilling to make the leap of faith."
>
> —JAMES CAMERON

Shari quickly became the most high-profile female manager in MMA and achieved groundbreaking accomplishments on behalf of her client. Her first priority was to renegotiate his contract so that his compensation would be commensurate with his accomplishments and the drawing power that she was focused on building. Then, not only did she secure first-time MMA sponsors such as Gatorade and Under Armour, she also convinced CAA, one of the premier sports and entertainment agencies, to represent her client.

Shari stepped into the unknown when she started to work in the MMA field. "I did not know how to be a manager; I just figured it out as I went along."

"Figuring it out" got Shari the very first Manager of the Year Award that the MMA awarded in 2008, and she received it again in 2009. According to MMAPayout.com: "While her accomplishments speak for themselves, Spencer accomplished it all as a woman, emerging as a leading voice in a male-dominated industry. Furthermore, her willingness to work with CAA showed a personal sense of security and commitment to her client's best interest above all else that is rarely seen in the management business in or out of MMA."

HUNGER

Shari's game is a perfect example of what happens when the game comes to you. She didn't start out with a hunger to be an award winning Mixed Martial Arts manager, but she did have a hunger to help others in their businesses. The fact that she worked with the MMA athletes was not a plan of hers. When she thought back on her internal motivation at the time, she said she didn't recognize how bored she was doing what she was doing, performing financial analysis and pro forma projections for investment banking transactions, until she did something that she never saw herself doing, never imagined she would be doing, but fell in love with the work and her clients.

"My motivation and my desire were doing what was best for the fighter. They didn't always know what was best for them because of their lack of experience in the ways of business. This was obviously because their focus is on being the best fighter they can be in all the various martial arts disciplines that they study. They are wrapped up in being the best fighter. I wanted them to have the best representation that they could as they prepared for their retirement."

In essence, she hungered to help these athletes to be their best.

COMPELLING PURPOSE

Shari managed these athletes for the benefit of moving them forward and helping them prepare for a change in their lives. Her business model was to always ask herself the question, "Does this serve this athlete's life purpose?"

As she learned more about this field, Shari saw that there were other managers who had drastically different business models from her own, and in a few cases acted in ways that appeared to be more in the manager's best interest than the fighter's. In many cases a manager might have a large roster of fighters to manage, limiting the time available to focus on any one fighter's brand development or business interests. Or, rather than having a long-term strategy, they focused on immediate opportunities that provided money in the short term, but may or may not have been in the fighter's best interest in the long run.

"It was very easy for me to make decisions; I turned down high-level sponsorships that I didn't believe in because it didn't fit with the fighter. It may have been money in their pockets, but if it didn't benefit my client or his brand in the long run, then it didn't make the cut. Protecting their brand was always the compelling purpose, because through their success, I became successful. I never had to focus on me; it was always about them. This other focus came naturally to me. If I ever found myself deviating or wondering what to do, that was always my benchmark."

> "Open your eyes, look within. Are you satisfied with the life you're living?"
>
> —BOB MARLEY

COMFORT ZONES

When I asked Shari what comfort zones she had to leave, she said, "This is the easiest question to answer. Everything was out of my comfort zone. My comfort zone was building financial models on Excel spreadsheets. I will actually test my Excel skills against anybody, any day of the week."

Because this was a completely new and unexpected field to her, she had to learn things such as what a signature was worth on a trading card; what an athlete should be receiving for his sponsorship; and all about brand development. "It was all new, but I thrive in an environment where I am challenged, typically where it is over my head and it is a stretch. That motivates me and challenges me."

Shari also had to leave her comfort zone often because of the people with whom she was negotiating at the table. "At one point, we were renegotiating a fight contract for Georges. The gentlemen that owned the promotion (the UFC), also owned multiple casinos, and were on the cover of *Forbes* magazine, and I am sitting across the table from them in negotiations. At that moment the thought crossed my mind, 'Who do I think I am doing this?' I took a deep breath and told myself that as long as I was doing what was best for Georges, I was more than adequate to be sitting there. I familiarized myself with the negotiation process and did my homework to know what he was worth. Even though I was uncomfortable, and I was nervous, I am very proud to say he ended up getting ten times what they originally offered. This experience stretched me and made me stronger than if I was still building spreadsheets and was bored out of my mind."

> "When I stand before God at the end of my life, I would hope that I would not have a single bit of talent left, and could say, 'I used everything you gave me.'"
>
> —ERMA BOMBECK

GULP

Just stepping into the role of being an MMA manager was a very big gulp for Shari. She knew that Georges was taking a risk (a gulp) by placing his faith in her, asking someone who had never managed before to manage him. "He had the belief that my having over twenty years' business experience would put me in a better position to represent him than someone who had more experience managing fighters but limited business experience. In retrospect, I think this experience made me a stronger manager. I brought in a different perspective, a more unique perspective and approach that a lot of the other managers did not have.

"The other time, obviously, was the time I spent negotiating with the people on the cover of *Forbes*. That was very intimidating.

"Being interviewed was also a big gulp for me. I had to get comfortable with this, as it's a big part of managing any professional athlete. I had to do radio and television interviews when he wasn't available. Seeing my name on ESPN.com and SI.com and that whole idea of becoming comfortable that every word you say is being recorded. That was a big gulp for me."

BOLD ACTION

Shari knows that every time she feels a gulp she is taking a bold action. For her, when she would step forward and move outside her comfort zone and take that gulp, it was, in addition to being a bit scary and frightful, extremely exhilarating. "Taking bold actions was motivating for me. It was the thing that would make me get up before my alarm went off in the morning. I felt driven. I have a very strong moral compass and there were times that I stood up to organizations that were much bigger than me. I didn't always make them my friends, but the reason I was taking a stand against a big organization was based on a moral stance and for no other reason. I took bold actions because that is what I believed was the right thing to do."

> "Here is the test to find whether your mission on Earth is finished: if you're alive, it isn't."
>
> —RICHARD BACH

ASK YOURSELF . . .

- Shari's game "found her." In other words, she didn't have a strong pull to this field to begin with, but through her experience and an invitation from Randy Couture to work with her, becoming an MMA manager became her bigger game. What in your life may be a bigger game that is looking for you?

- Shari knew that to take a bold action was preceded by a gulp. For her this gulp felt scary, frightening, and exhilarating all at the same time. What was the last gulp you felt and what did it feel like?

- What is the next gulp you must feel for the sake of your game?

Chapter 9

....

LINDA ALEPIN, FOUNDING DIRECTOR OF THE GLOBAL WOMEN'S LEADERSHIP NETWORK

....

Bigger Game: Create Women Leaders
Around the World

In addition to her role at the Global Women's Leadership Network (GWLN), Linda Alepin was Santa Clara (California) University Dean's Executive Professor of Entrepreneurship. She believes the game changers for the twenty-first century are women. As women step into being the most powerful leaders they can be, there will be major strides toward peace, environmental sustainability, and prosperity.

Linda's Bigger Game is creating women leaders around the world. Her favorite quote, by futurist Joel Barker, is "Vision without action is merely a dream. Action without vision just passes the time. Vision with action can change the world."

> "Women are the real architects of society."
> —HARRIET BEECHER STOWE

She knew that meeting the basic requirements of survival and independence is a significant challenge for many women in the world. Fifty-seven percent of the world's population lives on less than $2.50 a day; most are women and children. Centuries of male-dominated cultures have taught women to be powerless. The Global Women's Leadership

Network exists to help women around the world step out of survival and dependence into their inherent power and thus transform their worlds.

Linda founded GWLN based on the intention to work with women, in partnership with men, to create an environment conducive to broad participation for major social change. GWLN's leadership program builds the capacities of leaders all over the world. The graduates create networks of trust, respect, collaboration, and friendship. GWLN strives to ensure inclusion, innovation, and long-term focus while teaching transformational and ethical leadership practices.

> "Don't let the noise of other people's opinions drown out your inner voice."
>
> —STEVE JOBS

One of the things that made Linda successful in this endeavor is her total dedication to the development of those around her. She believes that people are pure potential, and that given experience and mentorship, they can take on incredible challenges.

Linda lives her life like the tagline of GWLN: Whole Woman, Whole Leader, Whole World.

HUNGER

In 1996, Linda was involved in an early Internet start-up. She was the founder and CEO and also the primary mover of the company. On her way home after a particularly tough day, she stopped to take a walk in a local park, because she was not quite ready to be the loving mother that she knew her family expected when she got home. On her walk she found a spot by a stream under some trees. She stood there trying to get quiet. As she settled, a picture of women from all over the world coming together to learn about leadership and being held together by the Internet came to her. That became her vision and was the beginning of the Global Women's Leadership Network.

It took eight more years for the organization to actually get started. She kept that vision alive by speaking of it often and speaking of it widely. Eventually, her friend Barry Posner of Santa Clara University said, "It's time."

"I rose to the top of the corporate world as an officer of a Fortune 200 company. I am still often uncertain about what to do in my life, but what I am certain about is that women from around the globe will create a new future for humanity. For me, this is what it is all about; more women stepping into their power."

COMPELLING PURPOSE

Linda believes in the power of women. She believes that there is an emerging calling and a yearning for women's leadership style. The reason women have not stepped into more powerful roles in the world is in part because they haven't had the opportunity; another reason has to do with society's pressure to keep them in traditional roles. The key roles for women in the past have been to take care of the home and children. Many societies have limited the legal rights and opportunities for women more than they have for their male counterparts. In today's world, more and more opportunities are opening to women in the workforce and in the political arena. The concept of women being in leadership roles is becoming a very compelling and beneficial notion.

Linda is not certain precisely when she became a leader, but she can point to a specific milestone, back when she was working at IBM, when she found a mentor. One manager looked at her and he said, "You are going to take my place as a manager within five years." So there it was: the challenge. Linda has always lived up to challenges that were thrown at her to keep moving up in leadership.

Linda loves James Kouzes and Barry Posner's book, *Encouraging the Heart: A Leader's Guide to Rewarding and Recognizing Others.* She cites a section in the book where Barry and Jim are talking about the "dark days" when one is finding one's own voice. They say that one day you are tired of saying someone else's words and you wake to a new power of finding your own voice and saying what you, yourself, believe. "I believe this is the ultimate challenge for women as leaders. We must begin to speak our own truth and live our own words."

COMFORT ZONES

Linda is a natural "doer." She is very talented—whether programming in her early career or working on strategic development later on. She had the idea of a global women's network and imagined what it could become. "Creating this would never have happened if I had not left my 'doer' comfort zone and enlisted other people's help. I still have this tendency to do things myself, so I am always consciously leaving this comfort zone."

Another challenge to Linda's comfort is asking people for money. The whole idea of asking for money is hard for her. Of course, that is fundamental to funding GWLN or almost any organization. So she had to leave her comfort zone of earning everything herself to relying on others to give of their resources. Linda took a hard, in-depth look at the value of what GWLN was doing. From both a personal and an organizational viewpoint, that inquiry framed her asking for money in a different way. "I took the personal out of the asking and I was no longer shy about touting the value of what was happening. I kept thinking of the women this money would help in making them leaders in their communities."

> "The day will come when men will recognize woman as his peer, not only at the fireside, but in councils of the nation. Then, and not until then, will there be the perfect comradeship, the ideal union between the sexes that shall result in the highest development of the race."
>
> —SUSAN B. ANTHONY

Once again, a book inspired her: Lynne Twist's *The Soul of Money*. As Lynne espouses, asking people to contribute to worthy causes is actually a gift and allows life's force to flow through them.

Linda has had to continually step out of her comfort zone of being complacent with the status quo. She has pushed to run the program again and again. She had to develop organizational structures and a business model where GWLN could find funding over a period of years. "My challenge today? What's the next comfort zone I must step out of? I need to leave my comfort zone of holding the program in the US and take it to India and beyond."

GULP

There have been several gulps along the way for this courageous woman. It was decided to make GWLN 100 percent independently funded. GWLN set a goal to raise all of the funds itself to be self-sustaining, and that was a big gulp.

Another was when the organization moved from the concept of a local women's center to an international women's network. There were no models of global networks in 2005. The technologies to accomplish this were primitive at best. So, for Linda, there was a gulp in developing a global women's network. This was a concept that has now evolved to encompassing a global cooperative.

"When you are taking on the whole globe, there are a lot of gulps. I have learned to decide what I am committed to and then to move forward towards that goal. Gulp or not."

BOLD ACTION

"One of our biggest bold actions we experienced was when we first started. It was to put the word 'global' into the organization's name. We were thinking of calling ourselves simply the Women's Leadership Center, but we said 'No.' We wanted to go global. That was a really big thing. It was a bold action and a gulp. The other gulp was giving up on the idea of being a 'center' and conceiving of being a 'network.'"

Linda remembers when she first presented this idea to the advisory board at the Santa Clara Business School. One of the comments was, "Could you pick a larger market segment?"

GWLN's first bold move was to hold a daylong leadership conference. Here was an organization with no reputation, no history. That day 235 people came to hear about the new organization and sample the leadership training. The conference provided the positive reinforcement that was necessary for implementing the program and signing women on.

Early on, GWLN used the Santa Clara University alumni newsletter and the Stanford University alumni

> "If you have knowledge, let others light their candles in it."
>
> **—MARGARET FULLER**

newsletter to get the word out. Amazingly, there were soon responses saying "I am coming" from countries including Uganda, Mexico, Indonesia, and many, many more.

Linda credits the power of her voice to getting the organization started. "There is bold action and power in just voicing an idea."

ASK YOURSELF . . .

- Linda found her bigger game on a walk in nature that allowed her to let go of the everyday pressures of her different roles. Is there a place you can go to stop "doing" and just "be"? When will you go there? Put it on your calendar. Even better, put down this book and go now.

- "There is bold action and power in just voicing an idea." Linda believes this, and for eight years before GWLN was formed, she spoke and spoke and spoke about her idea. What do you need to begin speaking about? Who do you need to speak it to?

- One thing Linda has learned along her journey is that she decides what she is committed to and then moves forward toward that goal. "Commit" simply means to dedicate yourself to a certain course of action. What are three things you will commit to right now? Be sure it is something you can carry out. Don't set yourself up for failure. Commit to what you can do.

Chapter 10

·················

ALL ABOUT THE BIGGER GAME: INVESTMENT PIECE

In Chapter 2, I stated that after the seven game-changer story chapters —where we focused on The Bigger Game model pieces of Hunger, Compelling Purpose, GULP, and Bold Action—there would be one chapter each for the four generic model game pieces of Investment, Allies, Sustainability, and Assess. The following four chapters take a deeper look at what these women had to invest in to make their dreams, visions, and games real.

The Investment piece is the place on the game board where we really ante up. This is where we start investing in the most critical and valuable asset of our bigger game: ourselves. The Bigger Game Player. The Game Changer. Remember, a bigger game is one that stretches you to be your very best. You need to develop new capabilities, learn new skills, and expand your capacity to live with intention, which is simply to be determined to act in a certain way.

I have a caveat here. We as women have a tendency to feel that we must be fully prepared and 100 percent confidently knowledgeable about all aspects of something before we move forward or say "yes" to anything that may be a stretch for us.

Claire Shipman is a reporter for ABC News, and Katty Kay is the anchor of BBC World News America. In two decades of

> "Live as if you were to die tomorrow. Learn as if you were to live forever."
>
> —GANDHI

covering American politics, these two women have interviewed some of the most influential women in the country. They were surprised to discover the extent to which these women suffered from self-doubt. They write about this discovery in *The Confidence Code: The Science and Art of Self-Assurance—What Women Should Know.* They wrote an article for *The Atlantic* (May 2014) called "The Confidence Gap." When the authors were looking at a 2003 study in which female students rated themselves significantly below male students on scientific competencies, they said: "We were reminded of something Hewlett-Packard discovered several years ago, when it was trying to figure out how to get more women into top management positions. A review of personnel records found that women working at HP applied for a promotion only when they believed they met 100 percent of the qualifications listed for the job. Men were happy to apply when they thought they could meet 60 percent of the job requirements."

> "You don't learn to walk by following rules. You learn by doing, and by falling over."
>
> **—RICHARD BRANSON**

Right here, right now, I encourage you to begin whatever you want to begin without being 100 percent qualified. Write all your self-doubts on one piece of paper—or two or three—and tear it up or burn it immediately. Feel the gulp and do it anyway. Get gutsy and get going.

If you are 100 percent qualified and experienced and have no need to step into the investment piece, this is not a bigger game for you. It is quite simply the same old game.

You need to ask yourself these questions:

- *What do I need to start doing?* For one of my bigger games, the women's conference, I had to start learning how to fundraise and how to ask large organizations for $10,000 at a time. I needed to start talking about my game and asking for funding. I also find that many women simply need to start making time for themselves.

- *What do I need to stop doing?* Many people find that when they define the game they decide to play next, they need to stop doing what is not working for them. This may be letting go of some volunteer work, pulling out of certain relationships that are no longer serving them, or even leaving their current work situation for the sake of their game. Remember that for everything you are saying "yes" to, you are saying "no" to something else.

- *What do I need to learn?* A coaching client of mine decided to start taking business courses so she could acquire enough knowledge to start her own business; she knew she needed to leave her corporate job where she'd hit the proverbial glass ceiling. Another client had to learn presentation skills after she was promoted into a position that required her to present to the executives of her company and to key clients.

- *What assumptions and beliefs do I need to change?* One of the major beliefs I had to change was that "I can do it by myself, I don't need help." Changing that one belief alone has changed my life and let me find other people who want to help and who have the skills and strengths I don't. I now believe asking for help is a strength and not a weakness. Besides that, I find people are waiting to be asked. They are waiting for an invitation to play. They may share the same vision or a vision similar to mine, but they don't have any idea of where to begin to make their vision a reality.

I always took great pride in my ability to accomplish a lot. I was one of the fastest "Check it off, it's done" people I knew. During a leadership program I attended, I pulled aside the leader and told her, "I am getting impatient with all these people. They seem to take forever to come to a decision and want to just talk on and on and on." She looked at me and smiled. "Pat, I know that you are capable of accomplishing a lot. I've seen it. The place I think you need to look now for the sake of your leadership is the idea that maybe in your hurry to accomplish so much, to check things off your list so quickly, you haven't considered that what you are accomplishing might be very small. What if you were to be more open to others' ideas and input when you present yours? Perhaps what you accomplish would be much bigger."

She was right.

When I began to open up and listen and practice patience and being fully present and mindful, I was able to see more possibilities and became more aware of who the people were that might want to help me in playing a Bigger Game.

Can you see how changing this belief also helped me change an assumption I had? The assumption I had was that "No one will want to be a part of this. No one will want to help me."

Well, I learned that old assumption was very wrong. I have found over many years that people want to help each other and be a bigger part of each other's worlds. They just don't know how. And maybe we're just the ones to show them how by inviting them to help us make our bigger games real.

We can do it better, together. This is now my viewpoint.

I imagine that at this point some of you might be getting over-whelmed at the thought of bringing your Bigger Game into the world. You don't need to learn everything all at once. Dru, for instance, has clearly found that investment in herself and her business is never ending. As she said about learning how to grow and run a farm, "Investing in all the skills we had to learn has been great, and it is definitely an ever-continuing process. It didn't happen overnight at all. We have been very slowly piecing things together so it has been a slow investment. Patience with ourselves has been our practice."

Anne realized she needed to learn how to ask for help as she looked around and saw all that needed to happen—and continues to happen. Due to her very public position, Sandy had to learn all there is to know about media communications, an area that seems to change and morph daily in our high-tech world.

WAYS YOU'LL GET INVESTED

Throughout the many years I've worked with this model with other people and in my own life, I've seen that the Investment piece shakes down to five sub-pieces on the board. As I spoke to each of the Bigger Game women featured in this book, I noted that the same themes ran through their situations. I have chosen to label these sub-pieces:

- Education or Training
- Personal Finances or Finding Investors Fundraising)

- Time

- Mindset

- Communications

Let's move on and look at these sub-pieces in more detail, especially as to how our Bigger Game Players invested in their games in these areas.

Education or Training

This sub-piece is all about learning or elevating your skills. It can take place in a formal educational environment such as a university, where you may need to enroll in a program to gain the skills or credentials that are required for your game, or it may simply be taking a refresher course at a local community college or online.

Some of my clients are large corporations that have a full training department or some form of tuition reimbursement for their employees. Using this resource may help those playing bigger games inside of organizations.

This one sub-piece has the potential to incorporate the other four sub-pieces. If you decided you need some form of formal education to play your Bigger Game, it may affect your personal *finances* by requiring an investment of your money to attend school. Seeing how this can impact the sub-piece of *time* is pretty clear. A shift in *mindset* is needed, as there is a short-term sacrifice for a long-term promise. You need to have a different mindset to be able to persevere to the end result. And *communicating* what you may need while you are here is important. Whenever we add to our knowledge of a particular subject, we grow more confident in articulating the details about it. Such confidence results in the clarity with which we use what we've learned and apply it to our Bigger Game.

Dru invested a lot of energy into learning how to run a business. She had to learn everything from payroll to workers' compensation to managing human resources for a farm that now employs over fifty people.

"The learning process of farming was definitely an investment. With some things you can go to school to learn, or take an independent workshop, but farming is more of a long-term investment. It takes years sometimes to learn how to grow something or raise animals, so the educational component was a big investment, and it still is."

Shari also invested a lot of time learning about the Mixed Martial Arts business. "I would say the first six to nine months was my major learning curve period. I needed to learn everything about the business; from learning what is involved with the athletic commissions to making sure that my client was licensed to fight and passed all of his medical exams. I picked the brain of everyone I could. I had to find strategic advisors that could help me in those areas.

"Fortunately, I found out that with enough general critical thinking, I would know the questions to ask and who might be able to help me find that information. I didn't have the experience, but I was smart enough to ask for help."

Personal Finances or Finding Investors (Fundraising)

As many find out, a bigger game may involve a financial investment on your part. You may leave a higher paying job for one where there will be less income, or perhaps none at all for a while.

About her personal finances, Shari said, "There was certainly a financial investment at the beginning. I took a deep pay cut during that time to take that step and invest the time not only to learn the business, but to also find others who believed in my client's ability to perform."

You may not need to invest your own money, but may find allies who believe in what you're doing and are willing to invest. Shari knows this firsthand. "I had to turn down short-term money because it took time to secure those blue chip sponsors. I was confident I would recover this money because it would be paid back through my client's success."

Shari also invested in hiring other personnel. "Then there was an investment in staff because I took on more support personnel to allow me to provide that full-service business model and take on some additional fighters when I added on to my roster."

As Libby said, "One of our big investments has been our own financial contribution in this project. We are luckily able to do that and to be volunteers. And because of that, along the way we have been able to get more help. We have received stipends and grants and help that we didn't expect, and that has been very helpful."

Time

Time is always an investment when you choose to play your bigger game.

Shari knew that there would be a major investment in time up front to build the company before the rewards would be there. "At the beginning, it was an investment in time and brand building, but I always knew it would pay off. The investment in the short term paid off tenfold financially."

As Libby stated, "Also, our willingness to give our time and to make this a major full-time commitment has been an investment. This meant giving up other things that we might have done that one could say would be more fun. Like when my husband retired we said: 'Oh, this is great, now we can go camping every month and just hop in the car and go someplace beautiful and set up our tent.' But we have rarely done this. We have given up that traditional leisurely retirement idea. We have given up one lifestyle for this one, with absolutely no regret. It has been fabulous. And it's fun."

Mindset

Adopting a different mindset is crucial for the success of our games. This can be a do-or-die element. What happens when we begin to consider investing in our game? That quiet (or perhaps very loud) voice in our head starts to talk more and more loudly. It starts being not so nice or encouraging. When we start investing in our games, it becomes vociferous and starts planting all those doubts into our head. "Who do you think you are? You don't know the first thing about doing this. Why would you want to leave the safety and security of your life? Why would you want to leave your comfortable job? You can't live on a cut in pay." And on and on and on. This is when we just need to thank those voices for their valuable input and tell them, "Go away. You serve no purpose for me or my moving forward with my bigger game."

For Dru, it was taking on the mindset of a leader and all that comes with that role. "I had to learn how to be a manager and a leader. A lot of farmers manage their own farm, but when you start to have twenty or twenty-five people, you need to become a leader too. You have to invest in learning how to do that and how to do it well, so that people like being here and like working for us in the long run."

Linda says that the biggest investment she had to make in creating her Bigger Game was letting go. "You have to let go of who you think you are, because that image of yourself is probably not the mental model of yourself for your bigger game. In other words, we have so many mental constructs; you have to let go of preconceived ideas and models to accomplish what you want. You cannot achieve global citizenship without letting go of assumptions, old beliefs, and those things that are not working any longer. So the investment I continually make is trying to know that I create my own barriers and they are not insurmountable. The only limits we have are the ones we put on ourselves."

For Linda it was also about changing her mindset on how to lead a nonprofit organization versus leading a for-profit organization. Her philosophy here is that you want people doing tasks that they love doing. They also want to grow, so she often asks people to take on bigger games than they might have chosen to play themselves. Fortunately, the work of the Global Women's Leadership Network is compelling and impactful. Despite the turnover inherent in all volunteer-led organizations, GWLN has succeeded in growing their network of women leaders in forty-two countries.

Shari was stepping into a very heavily male-dominated environment. She had to invest in a new mindset and she needed to get tough fast.

Communications

Bigger Game Players are always talking and communicating about their games. They take on the role of influencer, talking about their games to find allies and ask for what they need. They speak about their games with an excitement and passion that are contagious. To some, this does not come naturally.

Anne knew she would have to become very extroverted to promote her idea. For an introvert who doesn't like meeting new people, this was daunting. She started to take workshops on public speaking and fundraising. She read voraciously on business, management, and leadership and learned over many years to speak up and speak out. She learned to speak her mind, mindfully. This is the investment that brought her to creating a global organization, one step at a time.

> "I am always doing that which I cannot do, in order that I may learn how to do it."
>
> —PABLO PICASSO

As Sandy reflected on what she had to invest in her new bigger game, she said, "One of my top investments is actively engaging my stakeholders and audience, whether one person or a thousand. With technology today, every few minutes we are distracted by our phones, text messages, instant messages (IM), emails, etc. It has become an art to keep and engage your stakeholders and audience. I always invest into how to reach them more effectively." In her position, Sandy is considered a public figure, which brings a lot of visibility and responsibility. Among many things, she had to learn about media presence and how to handle any question presented to her at any time in any situation. "In this position, I have to be aware and ready to answer any questions from the media and realize the impact my answer could have. This was another skill I had to learn. I am fortunate to be surrounded by trained professionals and coached on how to be an asset to the company.

"I think the biggest thing I've had to learn is how to influence. I am in front of executives, managers, employees, customers, colleagues, media, and many other public and private leaders. Learning how to influence at this level can be rewarding and inspiring."

Anne's bigger game was definitely one she had no idea how to play. A major investment for her was to learn to ask for help. Again, a challenge for an introvert.

"I don't hesitate to ask people what should I do or what they think I should do. I mean, I knew people in the corporate world, I knew people in the foundation world. If I didn't know how to do something, I called up somebody and asked."

INVEST IN YOUR LIFE

As you can see, these women all had to invest in some aspect of their lives when they knew there was no turning back from their bigger game. They knew they had to say "Yes!" to what was calling them. I think Courtney summarizes this piece when she says that her life journey to get to where she is was her investment. "Every step that I have taken, every position I have had, everything I have done has led to this place. I am investing in these life experiences. I accept challenging jobs and take them on to be the person I am. To be the person that comes to a place and asks, 'OK, are you going to jump off?' If I don't jump, how can I justify it? As a leader, I can't justify it.

"My life has been my investment. I had to do the inner work to get here, because me making a difference as a leader in the world is not about my stuff. In order to be a leader in the world, you have to be clean and you have to be clear. I am always looking at what the issues are and what holds me back. Because if I am certain that I am here to make a difference, then what is the work I need to do?"

This is a game. People love to play games because they don't know the outcome. This game does not come with a final script. It is your life.

There may be a sixth subcategory. This one is an investment that may be unique to your bigger game. Be open to what you need to invest in for the sake of your game. The ability to be open to newness and change can itself be considered an investment in your game.

When we step into the Investment piece, we may look at what we need to invest in and become overwhelmed. "There's too much to do! Where will I fit it all in? When will I find the time?" Or we run scared. "Who do I think I am to do this? Others are doing something just like it. Why is this any different than that? It'll take too long to get it done." Or perhaps we just plain hit a wall. "This will never, ever work. I can't do this by myself. People will laugh at me." Yes, some or all of these objections

> "Investing in your-self is the best investment you will ever make. It will not only improve your life, it will improve the lives of all those around you."
>
> —ROBIN SHARMA

and expressions of self-doubt might cross your mind, but find the courage to shut that voice down.

And I encourage you to go back to The Bigger Game model and intentionally step into the piece called GULP. When you do this, reconnect to your hunger. Reconnect to your compelling purpose. Picture it. Picture your end result. It is when you reconnect with your hunger and compelling purpose that you will realize and awaken to the fact that your investments will be worth the rewards.

If you ever doubt this, just reread the words of the seven women. They gave themselves the space to fail. They felt the gulp and took the bold action to keep moving forward and investing in their game and themselves. They left the comfort zones that were not serving them for the sake of their hunger and compelling purpose. And they learned how to ask for help and found their allies, which you'll do too.

ASK YOURSELF . . .

- Let's go back to the beginning of this chapter and look at the four questions I asked you to reflect on. In light of your being more familiar with the investment piece of your Bigger Game, ask yourself:

  - What do I need to start doing? What do I need to say "Yes!" to?

  - What do I need to stop doing? What do I need to say "No!" to?

  - What do I need to learn?

  - What assumptions and beliefs do I need to change?

- In playing your bigger game, what strengths can you build upon? (Note: Take the *StrengthFinders 2.0* self-assessment by Tom Rath to find out what your strengths are and to find suggestions on how to build your strengths.)

- What is the financial investment you need to make at each stage of your game?

- What are the skills you need to learn or sharpen and how will you learn them? By when?

- What is the next investment you need to make in your bigger game? In yourself?

Chapter 11

·················

ALL ABOUT THE BIGGER GAME: ALLIES PIECE

I must admit to you that this piece of The Bigger Game board is my favorite piece to stand in. This is because finding allies has been both my biggest challenge and my biggest reward.

As I mentioned earlier, I was the youngest of three children, my brother seven years older and my sister ten. By the time I came into this world, my parents had pretty much done it all. So if I wanted to do something with them, I had to be the one to ask, and their answer was usually "No," because they had done this before with my sister and my brother.

I also learned very early on that because my parents had only a middle school education, I didn't ask them for help with schoolwork. I did ask my sister and brother for help, but because they were so much older than I was, they pretty much left me to my own devices. After all, I was the "baby" of the family, and who wants to spend time with one of those?

What this taught me very early on was quite simply: Don't ask for help, because you won't get it. And since that was one of the beliefs I learned at a very young age, I never questioned it. It was my reality. It was a core belief.

That core belief didn't change until I discovered that in order to play a bigger game, I needed to ask others to step on the game board with me. I started to see, through my experience of inviting others to participate in my games or asking others if I could join theirs, that people are waiting to be asked. For many women this is a challenge because many of us think we must be strong. We must know the answers. We must show that we are confident. We must show that we are the ones who can take care of others while showing we don't need to be taken care of.

We don't need to do this any longer once we fully step into the Allies piece.

I have found through my own process that people genuinely want to help and that asking for help doesn't look like a weakness. As a matter of fact, I now consider it a strength.

WHERE WILL YOU FIND ALLIES?

Just as with the Investment piece of the board, the Allies piece comprises a number of sub-pieces. I've labeled these as follows:

- Family and Friends
- Naysayers
- Prospects
- Co-players
- Champions
- Experts

There are also other allies that come into play. Any one of the above can act as a "Come In and Remind Me" ally. These are the people that we ask to help us get back on track when they see that we are off track. These allies are sometimes the most critical, as these are the ones who support you regardless of anything else. These are the allies that you can be perfectly clear about asking to help you in this manner. Come In and Remind Me allies are needed when you fall into that pit of frustration or anxiety about the progress or some other disappointing aspect of your game.

I have a brainstorming (B.S.) group that serves this purpose for me. I'll talk about this group a little bit later.

I also have another group of women whom I call my mastermind group. We have named ourselves Brainy Gutsy Yippee Champs. Each one of these relates to our businesses. Brainy is Dana Wilde of "Train

Your Brain" fame (http://danawilde.com). Gutsy is my Gutsy Women Win (http://GutsyWomenWin.com). Yippee is Elizabeth Crook of Bigger, Smarter, Richer (formerly Discover Your Yippee) (http://biggersmarterricher.com). And Champs is Shari Spencer of The Spencer Firm (http://TheSpencerFirm.com). We met three years ago at a business seminar and have been meeting virtually every other week to discuss our business progress and what we can do to help each other. These are the phenomenal women who come in and help me keep moving my bigger game forward. They always remind me of who I am, and they have faith in my capabilities—and in me when I don't have faith in myself.

We can also find allies by being in nature or connecting with our spirits or even connecting with our spirits in nature. In this category are those things that help us get away from the work our game calls us to do and to take a break.

This includes getting up and getting out. Go for a walk in nature. Sit by the ocean and count the waves. Go for a hike. Just change your environment in some way. Nature is a big ally of Linda's. She gets rejuvenated from long walks and being in nature. If she hadn't been in

> "The best time to make friends is before you need them."
>
> —ETHEL BARRYMORE

nature that afternoon before going home, the idea of the Global Women's Leadership Network might never have come to her. Being still in nature gives us time to reflect.

Having faith in or believing in God or some form of a Higher Power serves as an ally for your game. As Courtney said, "I don't think you know when you step out of your comfort zone and begin your bigger game if people are going to follow or not. But you need to believe in your conviction and have faith that God will lead the way."

All resources that help you relax mentally, physically, and emotionally are allies that fall under this heading. When I need a break or find my brain to be a bit fuzzy and feel that things are getting harder, I meditate, do a little stretching, exercise outdoors, walk with a friend, listen to music I love, and even dance in my office. I try to get out of my mind. This helps me rejuvenate.

Another thing that fits here is our relationship with our animals. I have Maggie, a thirteen-year-old Bearded Collie. Maggie is the one that reminds me to take a walk, and every day, around 4:30 p.m., she comes and sits by my office chair and just stares at me. Relentlessly. I absolutely know it is time to wrap up what I'm doing and take her to the dog park.

She is a great ally of mine.

There is also the "other" category, which contains all those things that inspire and help us. I have been sending out a "Quote for Your Day" via email and my social media outlets for more than sixteen years now. Words are very powerful and I find these quotes are inspirational for me—so inspirational that I want to share them and hopefully inspire others. Every now and then someone responds to my post and says how a particular quote came at a really good time when they needed to know they were going to make it through something, or that it simply inspired them to get into motion where they previously felt stuck. Yes, words are also my ally.

For Courtney, Martin Luther King, Jr. is an ally. "He was willing to go out there and lead this incredible movement. He was a man who had faith to allow God to move in and through him and change the course of history."

Let's spend a little time taking a look at who in our lives might fit into the above categories of the Allies piece in our bigger game.

Family and Friends

These folks are pretty much a given to support you in your bigger game. These allies are the people who are already there for you—connecting you to resources, listening to you, and offering feedback. They admire who you are and what you are up to in the world. These are the folks who are proud of what you are doing and will always be there to give you some recognition, celebration, and "Atta-girls."

As I talked to each of the women in this book, they all had someone in this category they could easily and quickly name.

One of Dru's strongest allies has been family. "My husband Paul's family farms are near us. They were very helpful in lending us equipment and just providing us with infrastructure support. My mom has been a big ally because she has been coming to the farmers market every Saturday with me and helps to sell our produce. Having that support from your folks is great and has helped me sustain this business."

Sandy also feels very lucky to have grown up surrounded by great people. "My parents believed in me and inspired me to reach for the stars. Nothing was impossible. I have a sister who I admired for her strength, wisdom, and authenticity. I have had great class-mates who really helped me. I have had great bosses who have created headroom and provided me with great opportunities and learnings. I've had people open doors to allow me to get to people I couldn't get to on my own. Friends and teammates that were there every step of the way to ensure I succeeded when I doubted myself. These people have become my true friends."

> "Walking with a friend in the dark is better than walking alone in the light."
> —HELEN KELLER

Libby's children supported her and her bigger game co-player, her husband. "Our adult kids have cheered us on in this effort. Although they do not participate in this, they are always asking how it is going. They have always been very supportive of what we do."

Anne's life partner was a huge ally. "He invested almost the same level of intense commitment as I did." Her friends proved to be equally supportive. "I had dinner with two friends and they really helped cata-lyze my ideas. These two friends, another woman I had breakfast with that loved my idea, and I became the first four members of the Board of Directors. I was thinking, 'Let's create an organization,' and blurted out, 'Why don't you be on the Board?' It was just like that."

The good news about finding allies within your friends and families is that they only want the best for you. They want you to be safe, healthy, and happy. As you progress over your bigger game life span, they may get a little afraid that you will lose these things and they may start to question or even speak negatively about what you are doing. Listen to them. They may be saying something you really need to hear, but do not let them hinder your growth or put a pair of blinders on your vision.

Quite a few years ago, I was at a point in my business where I needed to infuse some new ideas into what I was doing. I wanted to find a group of people with whom it would be mutually beneficial to brainstorm.

I got together with a friend and shared my idea of finding such a group. She was interested, so we decided to check in with others we knew and see if we could gather eight people to meet regularly to brainstorm with us. We invited these folks and at the first meeting we decided on the process. We discussed the structure and decided everyone would get five minutes to present an issue or idea they would like the group to brainstorm on. The presenters then state their specific ask: what is the question they want the group's feedback on?

The group then gets two minutes to ask clarifying questions on the specific ask. Then it is opened for eight minutes for everyone to throw out ideas. No idea is shut down, and the presenter just listens to the ideas and can ask questions only for clarification. No excuses why it can't be done; no "I've tried that before." Just listen and ask for clarification. Two people take notes so the presenter doesn't need to worry about remembering the suggestions.

After seven years, my brainstorming group, or "B.S." group as we call it now, is still going strong. This is where *Gutsy Women Win* was fertilized and birthed and grew. Thanks to the "B.S." women's never-ending support, you are reading this book now.

Naysayers

Naysayers are the people in our life who pretty much attempt to kill our ideas. They can be competitors, road blockers, people who actually voice all the negative things our monkey mind is telling us. There are many reasons they may try to sabotage our moving forward in our games, but those reasons are not relevant. What is relevant is that you need to be able to say "thank you very much" and move on. As Courtney said, "It is as important to thank those that oppose you as it is to thank those that support you, because they are wonderful teachers that can lead you to becoming a better you, if you allow it."

For Dru, a "naysayer" ally was the university she attended, which taught chemical farming and not organic farming. Other naysayers were the farmers she sought out for advice early in her farming years. Thirty years ago there were a lot of statements like "You can't feed the world organically" and "It's a fallacy that you can do it without all these chemicals." It was a really big gulp for her to say anything in opposition to those farmers. But she did.

"Now it's fun," Dru says, "because we have the university begging us for tours so they can show people what we are doing. That was, and at times still is, a very big push for me. I enjoy just sitting back and going 'I told you so.'"

In her position in politics, Courtney knows that some of her biggest allies have been naysayers. She has grown immensely in learning how to respond to this type of ally. "Some people I thought would be on board with me ended up not being on board. I took this to heart, because that was hard. One of the darkest nights I had in this work was realizing the nastiness of some of the other elected leaders and how they were interacting and maneuvering with my position. I really had to get into my tears and get into my own space and had to grieve. I was grieving about this being where we were and that was how Oakland was operating. These types of interactions were not for Oakland's best. We were no longer looking at a common goal. We were engaged in the game of petty politics, but once I really understood this was what I was and [could] accept that and grieve it, then I could move forward in a way that I had not been able to move before. It was because I accepted it as is. Once I could do this, I could change it."

> "True friends stab you in the front."
> —OSCAR WILDE

In her book *Paradigm Found: Leading and Managing for Positive Change,* Anne included an entire section on naysayers. For her, these are the people who are negative about your ideas and say they can't be done or they're impossible. "In a start-up, at the very beginning at least, it is very important to either not associate with these people or instantly turn what they are saying into a to-do list of things that you can consider how to respond to when the same negative input comes from someone else."

Naysayers are important to Sandy's journey. "I think you need both supporters and naysayers as allies. If you depend on your trusted advisors and they are always saying yes, you are going to get too comfortable again and go back to your comfort zone. You need to balance it with the no's in order to push you."

Prospects

Prospects are the individuals who are or will be your target market. They consist of your current or future clients, customers, or constituents. These are the ones we serve in our game.

When Anne first started Global Fund for Women, the organization grew very quickly in terms of donors, advisors, grantees, volunteers, and people who wanted to come and help be a part of it. It was a very big challenge to manage it all, but she called all of these people allies. Everybody. "I found out what the organization meant to the people who were involved in it. I found out why they were dedicating their time, money, and brainpower. Their responses were very helpful in turning around and fundraising and getting more people involved because we knew what people wanted. It made it easy to prospect because the idea appealed to a great number of people."

Co-players

These people are allies who sign on to your game. They may be actual legal partners in your game. As Dru said, her husband is a co-player. Same investment. Same drive to succeed. Same purpose.

"After about five years of farming, we realized that to raise a family and meet one of our goals, which was to derive all of our income from farming and not have to work off the farm, was going to be hard. So we asked some other people to join us as partners. There are now four of us that own the business together. They are my co-players."

A co-player may be an ally who is your spouse or partner in life or someone who is very much committed to your compelling purpose.

When I decided that the "Women Seeing Beyond Today" conference was a bigger game I wanted to make a reality, I had many co-players who came to work on the organizing committee with the same dedication and drive as I had. These were the co-players for my game at that time.

Champions

Champions are the ones who cheer us on. These are the people in our lives who believe in our bigger games. These are the ones who are great to go to when you need a boost of confidence or someone to lift you up when you're feeling down.

Gayle, a good friend of mine, and I have agreed that whenever we feel really pulled down, or let someone or something get to us, we pick up the phone and call the other one. All we say at the beginning is, "Tell me three things that you love about me." Or "Tell me three things I am really great at." Then we just listen. At the end of listening to someone tell us some pretty wonderful things about ourselves, we simply say "Thank you" and move on. It's amazing how having someone say something nice to you can immediately change your mood and help you feel powerful again.

Champions are also those who volunteer their time and talent to your game. To have Libby's dialogues grow into what they have, she had a lot of champions and youths to mentor and learn from. "My champions are all the participants in the groups and there are many, many people who are as passionate about it as we are. They are all the people who go to the high schools and colleges and travel to other states for conferences and serve on the panels. These include the Palestinians and the Jews who come to share their stories. We have fabulous volunteers who do this work without payment. They just give themselves, their time, and their stories because they believe in this life. Believe me, this dialogue wouldn't be anything without these diverse people. There are many, many groups in the country and overseas that are sources of inspiration we connect with and consider our friends."

Linda has had many champions and advisors. Literally hundreds of volunteers have helped her build Global Women's Leadership Network. She believes that people who work with her are held together by their visions of what they want the world to look like.

Champions are also those people who model how we want to be. Courtney loves people and inspired leaders. There were some amazing allies along her political journey. As she said about one of them in particular, "Laura Chick, former auditor and controller of Los Angeles, is an ally of mine. She is very clear on what she is about, what is right, what is wrong, and what she is going to fight for. She is not afraid of pissing people off. When she was in office, her constituents called her 'the conscience of LA.' She is a model of what being in political service means for me."

Experts

These are the people who have the experience, skills, and knowledge to help us launch, build, and sustain our bigger games. These folks may include a business manager, accountant, web designer, social media expert, lawyer, etc. These are the individuals with specialized skills that help us play our bigger games.

Some really big allies for Dru are all the other local farmers in her cooperative. "We do a lot of knowledge sharing and cooperation, like trucking and purchasing cooperatively. I really feel that we would not be here if it was not for some of our other local neighbor farmers."

For Sandy there has been a huge investment on her part, not only working with media coaches and public relations experts, but also through asking for counsel from mentors and executives and other leaders who have gone through what she is now going through. "Their advice and leadership have been invaluable."

Shari had several mentors along her path to success. "There was a founder of one of the sponsors we worked with who took me under his wing, and I gained a lot of insight from him. There was another manager of a fighter that would share with me some of their best practices, in terms of how to handle personal appearances and autograph sessions. Then later, I was able to repay him in other areas with my experiences. He somewhat paid it forward with me. These mentors were few and far between, but they were there. I did have a support staff that I relied upon heavily to help me make sure that I was not dropping the ball in any area with regards to my clients."

Barry Posner, the world-renowned leadership author, is a big ally of Linda's. He would send her articles that

> "Keep away from people who try to belittle your ambitions. Small people always do that, but the really great people make you feel that you, too, can become great. When you are seeking to bring big plans to fruition, it is important with whom you regularly associate."
>
> —MARK TWAIN

always seemed to have the answer to a current dilemma and supported her in growing the Global Women's Leadership Network.

FINDING YOUR ALLIES

What I've learned about allies is that some are there already, like family and friends, but for most, it is best to strategically select your networks and allies for your specific game.

The great thing about finding allies is that you already have a network where you can either find an ally, or ask if they know someone else they could introduce you to that might be an ally. It's the two or three degrees of separation that can help you find the allies you need to impact and influence the changes you are seeking to make. It is surprising how allies will show up once you begin to talk about your bigger game. It is amazing, when you think of it, how we are all connected in some way, and that technology and social media have helped aid those connections. A simple post asking for a specific thing can bring many of these allies into your life. It is so much easier to connect and be a part of change than it ever has been.

> "Lots of people want to ride with you in the limo, but what you want is someone who will take the bus with you when the limo breaks down."
> —OPRAH WINFREY

Watch for the synchronicity to happen as you begin to speak about your game. Be aware that allies are all around you. You will find them in the most unlikely places. I have found allies at networking events, sitting in a coffee shop, talking to a person at a restaurant. All of a sudden you find connections and begin talking about your bigger game with such enthusiasm and conviction that others will want to join you and become allies. Just find the common ground and discover what makes them hungry. What is the compelling purpose they are yearning to live? You will be amazed how you find your other game players.

This is all about us helping each other find something greater than ourselves. We know we are all in this thing called life together.

I am a firm believer that every single person wants to make a difference in the world. They just don't know how.

Maybe, just maybe, you are the person to show them how. You just may be the person someone else is waiting for to show them a bigger game.

ASK YOURSELF . . .

- Draw a tic-tac-toe board and label the bottom of each of the pieces with the names of the nine categories of allies:
  - Family and Friends
  - Naysayers
  - Prospects
  - Co-players
  - Champions
  - Experts
  - Come In and Remind Me
  - Spirit and Nature
  - Other
- Think about the bigger game that you want to begin, or may now be playing, and put the names of the allies you can ask to be a part of your game in each of the nine categories. Make sure there is one name in each piece.
- On the above "ally" board, circle the names of three people you will call in the next twenty-four hours and ask to be an ally. Now, make those calls.
- Think of some things that naysayers may say about your game. Write down at least three statements. Now, write down your responses, in positive terms, to answer their statements.

Chapter 12

····················

ALL ABOUT THE BIGGER GAME: SUSTAINABILITY PIECE

The word "sustainability" has numerous meanings that relate to our environment, businesses, and resources. Merriam-Webster.com defines sustainability as "able to be used without being completely used up or destroyed; involving methods that do not completely use up or destroy natural resources; able to last or continue for a long time." Dictionary.com defines it as "the ability to be sustained, supported, upheld, or confirmed."

When I think of sustainability in the context of The Bigger Game, the definition centers on the person who initiates the game as literally the resource for her or his own game. As I often say, "Without me, this will not be."

For the purpose of our work here, let's define sustainability to mean that you accept responsibility for the long term of both your personal life and your bigger game. In *Play Your Bigger Game*, Rick Tamlyn says, "This position is about maintaining and building upon your game once it's up and running, which also includes self-maintenance so that you'll be around for the long term, too."

And who doesn't want to be around for the long term?

However, a word of caution here. Sometimes the games we play in our lives have the potential to leave us feeling overwhelmed, very

> "Take care of your body. It's the only place you have to live."
> —JIM ROHN

tired, or close to burnout. Sometimes our games cannot be sustained without a huge investment of energy and time from us. And still other games cannot be sustained because they are not sufficiently supported with enough of the right allies, or the game wasn't assessed in time to avert failing.

I know. Many times in my life I've had to give up a bigger game idea for the sake of my health and well-being. The Women's Conference ended because I made the decision that I did not have the time or the energy to work on it another year, even though it was something I was passionate about. Since there were no other allies that wanted to take it over, this game ended. I assessed the likelihood of it moving forward and decided I had to let it go. As with all things, I realized that it had its time and served its purpose. It was sad to realize that the game itself was unsustainable, but for the sake of my own sustainability, I had to let it go.

> "Take care to get what you like or you will be forced to like what you get."
>
> —GEORGE BERNARD SHAW

Here's one of the wonderful things about being a Bigger Game Player. You *don't have to sacrifice yourself* for the sake of your game. As a matter of fact, if you do, you can no longer play your game. Your game should energize you; it should bring you happiness and make you want to take care of yourself for the sake of continuing to play your game.

SUSTAIN YOURSELF

There's a wide range of ways you will find to sustain and take care of yourself. Just listen to the variety of ways some of the women included in this book cared for and nurtured *themselves* for the sake of their game. Several women mentioned yoga practice or reliance on friends as keys to their self-sustainability. For the sake of brevity I haven't repeated that, but I wanted you to know that certain means of sustainability are very popular.

Dru believes, "Eating well definitely sustains me. Going out and being able to pick a big bowl of strawberries right outside your back door is probably the biggest treat that anyone could ask for. Being able to have all this good food around us is wonderful. The farmers market sustains me because I get to connect with all the people eating our food."

Linda has been a practitioner of yoga for many years. She views yoga as one of the things that sustains her both mentally and physically. She also plays golf once a week, getting her outdoors, which she loves. "My work itself is inspiring and sustaining." When Linda gets to spend time with these women leaders and sees the work they are doing in the world, she is humbled and inspired to keep going.

Libby says the key to sustainability is having flexibility with her time, a good balance in her life, and the realization that there needs to be other things besides the work. "We are able to work out of our house. This allows us to have the leisure of going to bed and getting up when we want. We work out and grow veggies, go for walks, and go to movies. Sometimes sustainability is hard because when we are on a roll with our work, it is hard to stop. We now know that we just can't do this work twenty-four hours a day, seven days a week, and know how to pace ourselves."

> "Women in particular need to keep an eye on their physical and mental health, because if we're scurrying to and from appointments and errands, we don't have a lot of time to take care of ourselves. We need to do a better job of putting ourselves higher on our own 'to do' list."
>
> —MICHELLE OBAMA

Courtney answered the question of how she sustains herself this way: "What sustains me is my spiritual practice and my faith. My faith has been my underpinning for all my life. I keep a really clean body and regularly work out. Building up stamina is important in this work and a couple of years ago I started Pilates and boxing. It is real important to have a solid core. This work gets tough and you can feel some people go at your core. So I am grounded in my spiritual practice and grounded in my body."

Sandy shared that "a wake-up call came to me early in my career when I went in for my annual physical. I found not only my blood pressure was off the charts, but also my overall health was being compromised. I knew I had to make a lifestyle change. I began to exercise frequently, eat healthy, and take time off to reflect and rejuvenate. Every year I take two to three weeks off and go somewhere to spend time with family and friends. It not only strengthens our bond, but it gives me back my energy and quest for adventure."

> "To experience peace does not mean that your life is always blissful. It means that you are capable of tapping into a blissful state of mind amidst the normal chaos of a hectic life."
>
> —JILL BOLTE TAYLOR

Anne sustained herself through finding others to confide in. "I had a partner during that part of my life that was really there to listen and provide advice and reassurance. Allies would come in at the right moment to make sure I could get to the next level in my game. Those I could talk very openly with made me feel less alone. I began to look after myself and took a vacation every year. I also loved my work. That was the most important thing to keep me going. I felt compelled to do this work. I could not *not* do this."

Shari brought up the point of financial sustainability. "From a financial perspective, there was an initial investment of my unpaid time and a significant dip in revenue generated as I got started. But then, even as the fruits of my labor started to pay off, I kept myself living well below my means. In other words, I didn't change much of my standard of living. So that allowed for sustainability financially."

SUSTAIN YOUR GAME

There is sustaining and taking care of you, the player. There is also sustaining your game and how you can keep it going—sometimes even without you.

Anne had to make the tough decision a few years ago to retire from the Global Fund for Women organization. "The process of growing GFW was a very creative act. I believed we were creating an organization as a work of art. Creating a work of art is part of my sustainability. But the main thing is, when I think of sustainability, I think of something being able to continue to go forward without me. I have always had a lot of energy. However, a few years ago, I began to notice I was getting tired and I wanted to do other things with my life. The organization was at a point where I wanted it to be. I was tired of some of the challenges and believed there were other good people that were able to continue the growth. I retired when the organization really looked great and it was in great shape. I think the way that you ensure that kind of sustainability for something to continue without you is extremely good planning. You have to plan for that type of transition. I planned for a transition that was not only easy financially, but also organizationally. The financial plan was that we had almost two years of support when I left. So anyone coming in could easily have run it for two years without worrying about the financial or organizational support having to change immediately."

Dru considers her family a key part of sustaining Full Belly Farms as well as educating the next generation on the joys and challenges of farming. "I think another thing that sustains me is that my kids are involved in agriculture now that they are growing up. My daughter is running a summer camp at our farm now and wants to be an agricultural educator. So that sustains me, to know that it is going on into the next generation. One of the things we have done in the past is to have interns spend a year here. Over the years we have had over one hundred interns. To see them now farming and having gone on to Oklahoma and New Mexico, it is sort of this really neat trail of people that worked here and learned how to become farmers and are going on to farm. In that bigger picture, I definitely feel like my work is going to be sustainable.

"On a daily basis, I definitely get a lot back from what I do. Since school groups come out here, I do a lot of education of kids. Seeing the light in their eyes as they learn about farming and food and sustainability is very rewarding and keeps me going, for sure. The core of my being is so satisfied when I read an article in a farming magazine about organic farming. There was an article I read the other day that was written by an intern that had been here, and she is farming in Oklahoma and writing articles about farming. It is just so exciting to see the impact of what you do on future generations."

While Courtney was changing the landscape of local politics, she felt something was missing. "The piece that was missing was I did not feel my life was complete. Four years ago I knew I did not want to go through this life and not be a mom. I decided to adopt through the foster care system, a process called foster/adopt, and in October 2011, I had two precious boys move in with me, a three-year-old and a four-year-old. I adopted them a year later in September 2012. It is the best decision I ever made. Now I have these two amazing boys that give me joy, happiness, and perspective on what's really important every single day.

"At the end of the day it is all about our relationships, and are we serving one another in those relationships—whether those are family or civic. I can move mountains if I am in service to others, but if at any point I think it's about me and my ego, the mountain won't move. When I am clearly aligned with loving more deeply, giving more, and trusting, truly nothing is impossible—my boys are proof of that. It took almost two and one-half years to find a match in the foster-care system. If I ever doubt God, all I have to do is go into my boys' bedroom at night and see their sweet, peaceful faces. My boys sustain me and are the main reason I serve and want my bigger game of honest and ethical politics for the people to continue."

Sandy is another Bigger Game Player who realizes the importance of sustaining her game for the long run. "I am impatient by nature. I want things now. I have always been the one that says, 'Are we there yet? Are we there yet? Are we there yet?' and I still do it today. Sustainability is really important. I could work twenty-four hours a day, seven days a week if you gave me the opportunity. I need to remind myself it is a marathon, not a sprint. In the work I do, I have to look at it five to ten years out, and build the foundation and groundwork today to be able to realize the results and impact of the future. You need to be patient as this work takes a while to realize the behavioral changes you are seeking. I love what I do so I am not looking to retire any time soon, but I know that I need to continually take care of myself to do this work and to make the impact I want to. I am sustaining not only my team and myself, but also my work in the diversity and inclusion field."

> "Nourishing yourself in a way that helps you blossom in the direction you want to go is attainable, and you are worth the effort."
>
> —DEBORAH DAY

Linda is currently pulling back from some aspects of the day-to-day operations and working more on the vision and the business model for the organization. She knows that for GWLN to be sustaining, other leaders will have to be ready and able to carry it forward. She says, "It's all an evolution."

SUSTAIN, DON'T DRAIN, YOURSELF AND YOUR GAME

Your bigger game should not be draining. It should be energizing. Sustainability of the player(s) is of the utmost importance. The analogy of how to use an oxygen mask in the event of an emergency on board an airplane fits this game piece perfectly: the point during the safety briefing when the flight attendant says: "In the event of a loss of pressure in the cabin, an oxygen mask will automatically appear in front of you. To start the flow of oxygen, pull the mask toward you. Place it firmly over your nose and mouth, secure the elastic band behind your head, and breathe normally. . . . If you are traveling with a child or someone who requires assistance, secure your mask on first, and then assist the other person."

> "Love yourself first, and everything else falls in line. You really have to love yourself to get anything done in this world."
>
> —LUCILLE BALL

Secure your mask first.

Breathe normally.

Take care of yourself for the sake of your game. If you do, your game will also take care of itself.

ASK YOURSELF . . .

- Are you physically, mentally, emotionally, and spiritually fit enough for this game? What do you need to do to become fitter in each of these areas?

- When you find that you are getting burned out, what is the next action step you can take?

- Look at your calendar over the next two weeks. What is it that you can do to help sustain you? Schedule it. Do it.

Chapter 13

·················

ALL ABOUT THE BIGGER GAME: ASSESS PIECE

Assessing is not judging—yourself, your allies, or your bigger game. It is not about criticizing yourself or your team for a lack of progress. It is all about taking an honest look at where you are, without judgment, and determining whether you will continue along the way or change your direction. It's that simple.

Merriam-Webster.com defines assess as "To determine the importance, size, or value of (assess a problem)." Assessing is the ability to look at what we are doing in our games as objectively as possible. It is hard; I don't believe we can ever be totally objective since we are always involved in what we are doing, hence it is always subjective and personal. But I think we can give our bigger game a pretty good evaluation, especially if we find allies to help us.

Assessing is not voting. Voting in this context implies that one has lost objectivity and has a view that is usually clouded by one's history of a certain experience or feeling. A vote often means that a view has been distorted by emotions; it doesn't look at data that can help us make an informed, objective decision. Voting is really laying your judgment and emotional reaction over "What is." Voting often means thinking it is good or bad, right or wrong.

Assessing is not taking a look at what we are doing in our bigger game and then judging ourselves for our lack of progress or our inability to do something or to find the right resources. It is about taking an honest and open inventory of where our game is and the direction it's going.

It is about evaluating from a neutral perspective. Assessing is all about taking a look at the data without the emotional charge.

Every bigger game must have a definition of success and a method of measuring success so that you, the player, can at any moment assess your progress. Just as a store takes monthly inventory, so must we take an inventory of our games.

WHAT ASSESSING LOOKS LIKE

Perhaps this example from my own experience will shed some light on the process when you're standing in this game piece. You'll come back to it again and again, believe me.

When I was playing my bigger game of the "Women Seeing Beyond Today" conference, my team and I were assessing all the time. We asked ourselves some of the following questions:

- Were the right co-players in place to get this done? Did we need other resources to round out the committee's skills? Did we need some more assistance from other resources? What was missing?

- Had we solicited the right speakers? Did we have the right speakers for our workshop categories? Would they provide the content we thought would best serve our attendees?

- Had we chosen the right channels for advertising? Was our message getting out to the audience we were targeting? Was our message enticing enough for women to register and attend?

- Did we have the right vendors? Were the vendors representative of the products we thought would benefit our attendees? Were the vendors in alignment with our vision and goals?

- Did we have enough funding? Did our budget include all the categories that we needed to be sure we were covered? Did we have enough in our budget to provide scholarships to the women who were unable to pay? How many women could we offer scholarships to?

Many questions were asked to determine what was best for the game.

A few years ago, playing another game, an associate and I had decided that we wanted to offer a women's leadership program inside large organizations. We met weekly, and all along the way we kept assessing who our audience was, what organizations this program would be good for, what materials we needed, what our pricing would be, etc.

We started to notice that there were longer and longer times between our meetings and we were not fulfilling our commitments to each other on a timely basis. We finally had to ask ourselves if we were the right co-players for this game. In the end, we decided we were not, so we let the game go and moved on.

USING THE MODEL TO ASSESS

As you play your Bigger Game, you will keep assessing along the way. "How's the game going? Is this the right game to be playing now? Where am I in the overall plan? Do I have the right allies? What do I need to invest in? What's my next bold action?"

One of the things I have next to my desk is a copy of The Bigger Game model. When I am assessing my game, I look at the model and think of which piece or pieces I'm standing in at that moment. I then think of where I need to go next to move my game forward. It's a great tool to determine what the next step is for me.

I look at my game and connect with the foundational pieces of Hunger and Compelling Purpose. I may realize that there is a Comfort Zone that I need to let go of, or a new Comfort Zone I have taken up and need to Assess. Perhaps I am feeling a big GULP and am not taking the Bold

> "Change is a continuous process. You cannot assess it with the static yardstick of a limited time frame. When a seed is sown into the ground, you cannot immediately see the plant. You have to be patient. With time, it grows into a large tree. And then the flowers bloom, and only then can the fruits be plucked."
>
> —MAMATA BANERJEE

"My feeling is if you're going to be a leader, you have to carefully assess where people are and where people want to go."

—HILLARY CLINTON

Action I need to take. There may be an Investment that I need to make that I'm not making. Perhaps I need to talk to an Ally to get input or support. Perhaps I'm feeling a bit burned out and need to Sustain myself for a few minutes, or hours, or days. Maybe I need to spend some time in reflective Assessment to see if there is something more to be done to Sustain the game. Perhaps I need to do one or more of these. Or—just maybe—I need to do all of these.

A major part of being successful in openly assessing your game is trying to be as objective as you can. Assessment is a place where you need to stay open to the possibilities and synchronicities that will appear as you play your bigger game and talk about it with others. Assessing with data and objectivity opens up possibilities. Voting, which brings in judgment and old emotions, limits possibilities.

Stay open.

OTHER ASSESSING TIPS

Dru invests lots of time in assessing her game. "All four of us partners have a yearly retreat. At this retreat, we assess not only the health of our business, but we also assess our own health. We lead very crazy lives and most days are fourteen-hour days. We assess how we are all doing and ask if we are able to keep doing this. We sit back and ask ourselves, 'Is this still fun for us? Are we getting too tired?' So far, it's still fun."

For Courtney, assessing is a very natural act. "I think that assessment is always a part of what I do. For me it is always about impact, impact, and impact. People ask me where I want to go next, and I know this role I am in is critical. I know I can make a difference, and I am always willing to go where I can make the greatest impact. So when I determine that I can make a greater impact somewhere else, I will leave. Assessing comes in when I have those really challenging days, and I ask myself if this really is where I am supposed to be. Right now, the answer is always yes. This is it for right now. I have got more work to do here. We are making an impact in relation to the culture and the integrity of this city and what I believe is a linchpin in getting this city over the hump. And then the next assessment will be asking myself if it is time for me to move on to the next thing and check to see if I'm in a comfort zone. Am I staying here because I am comfortable, or is it time for me to look at those fears I'm feeling and ask myself if I am still playing a bigger game?"

Libby also does a lot of assessing along the way. "We do a lot of soul searching throughout the day, and in the core dialogue groups we assess where we are and where we're going. Some of the other dialogue groups do it too. We look at what we can do differently and how can we reach out. We ask, 'Is there more?' We are always assessing and making plans for our next steps. We need to determine when to move forward and when to pull back. There's a movement and then a rest.

"In 2004, we said we really need to do something more creative to get out there, and someone said do a cookbook—and we did. We put together this fabulous cookbook, *Palestinian & Jewish Recipes for Peace*. We included the important information about dialogue and some wonderful stories about the participants and where they learned to cook and what food and life means to them. We sold well over a thousand copies. We assess what we need and how can we keep reaching out further and further."

For Sandy, her last job was a perfect example of assessing. "I had done that job my whole life and I was proud of what I and my team had accomplished, but I was waking up every morning with something missing in my life. It was that little voice in my head that kept building and pressuring me until it really smacked me. I started to really take a look at where I was, and ask myself if this was what I really wanted to be doing five years from now. Even though everyone else was telling me that the money and the title were going to make a difference in my life, I had to answer that question for myself.

"A close friend made it reality when she said that she felt there was something bigger for me beyond the current work I was doing. Through her urging and my assessing, it gave me the motivation to break out and follow my passion, despite many telling me that I was crazy to pursue this work. Big change starts with that little voice in your head starting to question. That voice is there for you to really take a hard look and do a full assessment of yourself and not just what people think you should be doing. You have to look at multiple aspects of it too. It really got me to stand up and say I am tapping out. It is a bold move and it is a hard move to leave some place that is comfortable. There are days I look back and say was I crazy to leave my previous position, but I still know, deep in my heart, that what I am doing right now is what I must do. And I keep assessing too."

Anne considers assessing taking an inventory of where you are. "We did the obvious kind of assessing. We asked ourselves, 'What are we learning? What do people think of us? What do the grantees think? Do they think we could do a better job?' The question we regularly visited was to keep asking: what is the basic mission of the organization? We had to keep assessing this, as the organization doubled in size every year for almost seven years. So the question is, how did we assess the work? Well, we did it in a routine, formal way. The way growing organizations should do it. The board would take time out every year and work on a strategic plan. We asked people what they thought. We asked ourselves, 'Are we doing what we set out to do? Should we be doing something different?' We asked ourselves the usual kinds of questions that you go through every few years or so.

"The interesting thing about GFW, to me, is that the organization is now over twenty-five years old and it is doing exactly the same thing it did early on, only on a larger scale. Our assessing always results in most everyone saying that this is a good idea and let's keep doing it. I think it is unusual in this way. It is a very simple but powerful global idea. We have money; they don't; give it to them to do good things. Be generous and be there for these people. I think the organization has become much more complicated, in the sense that it has become a very large organization financially and personnel-wise, but at some very basic level the idea of it is still a very simple idea."

Shari did a lot of assessing at the beginning of her game. "I had to

> "You have to have a clear picture of what is before you can make a wise decision on what's next."
>
> —RICK TAMLYN

assess, initially, whether I would achieve success by bucking the trend and doing things differently or doing them the same old way. I had to make the decision that was the way to go, and that my fighter was going to do his job inside the octagon. That criticism occurred in the early days because I was doing things differently. In the end, we proved our strategy was definitely successful. At the time I was doing it, I was heavily criticized—until it paid off. That was the ultimate success. At that time, there was a lot of assessing as to whether or not I was doing the right thing. I was saying 'No' to some sponsors that were within the fight industry. I was waiting for those from outside the fighting industry to help my fighter achieve crossover status. I wanted people to know him outside of the Mixed Martial Arts niche because I saw his potential to reach a broader audience. This strategy ultimately paid off, but there were constant assessments of the direction we were heading into along the way."

In assessing Global Women's Leadership Network, Linda talks about sensing from the universe and using her instinct about what's not working and what is. She says she can usually feel when the organization—or herself, personally—is in flow. "This happens when great coincidences come along and things flow. This flow tells me I am going in the right direction. The fact that GWLN is growing demands that we are always assessing some part of the program and the organization."

DO-BE-DO-BE-DO

My conversations with these women affirmed for me that assessing is critical to every bigger game. They revealed that assessment has two key components: being objective while you are assessing where your game is, and asking others for their input while assessing the game and the next steps.

> "We have so much room for improvement. Every aspect of our lives must be subjected to an inventory of how we are taking responsibility."
>
> **—NANCY PELOSI**

The women's experiences further revealed that there are two sides to assessment. One, the *doing* side, assesses the action and the state of your game. This is all about taking action and asking yourself, "How do I make this work? Is it working? Is it heading in the right direction? How can I grow this? Do I need to take a vacation from this game?"

Two, the *being* side, assesses your physical, mental, emotional, and spiritual state of being a player. This involves assessing what your perspective is at any point in the game and asking yourself, "Am I fully engaged? Is there still a compelling purpose pulling me forward? Am I still feeling the hunger? What comfort zones do I need to leave?"

Keep assessing. Keep asking yourself those difficult questions and answering honestly. Seek feedback from others and keep open to all feedback you receive. Answer all the questions you ask yourself when you stand in this piece of the game board honestly and openly. For the sake of your game, don't vote or judge. Be open to what your answers are.

ASK YOURSELF . . .

- Take a look at The Bigger Game model. As you look at the different pieces of the game board, where are you now? Assess. What piece do you need to take action on to move your game forward?

- Who are some allies you can find to help you assess as objectively as possible?

- Is the game that you are playing (or want to play) truly compelling to you?

Chapter 14

....

WHO ARE YOU BECOMING?

Once you have decided to play a bigger game in your life, your life will change. Be ready for it. Your game defines who you are becoming, so choose well.

When you choose to be a Bigger Game Player, your life will change, and this ability to be open to newness and change can itself be considered an investment in your game. You have just made a really big decision to leave those comfort zones that are no longer serving you. Feel the gulp playing a bigger game gives you, and do it anyway. It must happen. If not for you, who?

When you decide, consciously and with intention, to play a bigger game, you take on the role of a leader. People will begin to look at you in this light even if you never imagined this role for yourself. When I work with executives and leaders within organizations, one thing I remind them of is that people are always watching them for cues as to how they should react or respond to the situations they are in. When you play your bigger game, you consciously design a life for yourself that is engaging, dynamic, and full of inspiration for others. Leaders are always modeling behavior that their followers want to mirror. This is how culture is created.

People around you will begin to see you in a different light. Be ready

> "The thing that is really hard, and really amazing, is giving up on being perfect and beginning the work of becoming yourself."
>
> —ANNA QUINDLEN

for this. Your choice to be a Bigger Game Player will have impact and consequences. It can't help but happen. Certain people will want to come and be your allies. They will want to play the game with you, or support you in some way. Others, quite frankly, won't want to be involved at all and may slowly step away. Let them.

Many years ago I owned a fulfillment company with another woman and we applied for a "Best Customer Service" award from a top-tier international company. We were one of more than a hundred companies that entered the competition, and we won third place. At the award ceremony, the late John Wooden handed out the awards. For those like me who don't closely follow basketball, John Wooden was simply an American basketball player and coach. But for those who eat basketball statistics for breakfast, Wooden's record as the head coach at UCLA who won ten NCAA national championships in a twelve-year period—an unprecedented seven in a row—he was a god. One of the things he said that day was, "Success is peace of mind, which is a direct result of self-satisfaction in knowing you did your best to become the best you are capable of becoming."

This stuck with me, as I had been searching for my own definition of success. When I heard his words, I knew this was true for me. I knew that I would always be looking for things that used my skills, talents, and strengths. I knew that I would always do things that would be the best use of me. I knew that I want to be thoroughly used up when I die.

As George Bernard Shaw wrote in *Man and Superman*, in the "Epistle Dedicatory to Arthur Bingham Walkley" (1903):

> This is the true joy in life, the being used for a purpose recognized by yourself as a mighty one; the being a force of nature instead of a feverish, selfish little clod of ailments and grievances complaining that the world will not devote itself to making you happy.
>
> I am of the opinion that my life belongs to the whole community, and as long as I live it is my privilege to do for it whatever I can.
>
> I want to be thoroughly used up when I die, for the harder I work the more I live. I rejoice in life for its own

sake. Life is no "brief candle" for me. It is a sort of splendid torch, which I have got hold of for the moment, and I want to make it burn as brightly as possible before handing it on to future generations.

All of the amazing women included in this book changed for the better due to the games they chose to play in their lives. Sometimes they changed in unexpected ways, but they always changed. They always knew they were designing who they were becoming by moving their games forward.

Dru believes the size and quality of the game you play really does design who you are becoming. "When I started this dream of farming, I had this vision of homesteading. Me, a New Englander—picture that. Being a homesteader is what I thought I was going to be. Instead, I'm in California.

> "There is nothing of which every man is so afraid as getting to know how enormously much he is capable of."
> —SØREN KIERKEGAARD

I'm running this large organic farm with over fifty employees. I have definitely become a person that I did not have any idea that I would become at the beginning of my journey.

"I do still think that I am that New England homesteader in my heart, but in reality, I have become a business leader and owner, a successful farmer and farmwoman. This is the gist of it, this farm and my bigger game is what created me and who I am.

"I feel like I am becoming a spokesperson for women in agriculture. I seem to get a lot of people wanting to know what it is like to be a woman in agriculture. A lot of our interns are women wanting to start their own organic farms, so I also feel [like a] little bit of a spokesperson for the organic farm movement.

"Mostly though, I am becoming an educator, which I hadn't really thought I would be, but I love it. I love having kids and grown-ups alike come to the farm. I love talking to them about the farm almost as much as I love the farming itself."

Through educating others about organic farming, Dru is handing her torch to future generations.

Libby has a quote on her desk from Laurel Thatcher Ulrich that says "Well-behaved women seldom make history." Says Libby: "I have interpreted this to mean that a quiet woman or a shy or withdrawn woman rarely makes history. It's not like I am trying to *make* history, but I am trying to *help* history. I feel like my participation in creating these opportunities to dialogue about differences has enriched my life to the point that it has helped me see the whole of myself. It has helped me to become a more compassionate person, a better listener, and to have more nerve to stand up for what I think is important."

> "I feel myself becoming the fearless person I have dreamt of being. Have I arrived? No. But I'm constantly evolving and challenging myself to be unafraid to make mistakes."
>
> —JANELLE MONAE

Libby, along with her husband, is truly a Bigger Game Player who has made a big change in the world by simply creating the space for people to learn to be in conversation.

Not many people knew Courtney when she was running for Oakland City Auditor. "Even without a lot of people knowing me, I swept all the endorsements. I would say I swept the endorsements by being who I am. I love and respect people. I believe in them. I give people credit for who they are and the journey they have had." Others obviously saw this too in Courtney, as she won her election with 65 percent of the vote and is currently serving her second term after receiving nearly 67 percent of the vote.

Courtney also believes, "I am becoming more loving. I am becoming wiser and clearer. I finally get to be me. I am ready for whatever next step I take. That's who I have become. I said to some friends last night, 'I know that the woman that I am becoming will be a greater political leader.' I am allowing people to see who I am as a leader, to see what I am made of. This is the part where I am excited about who I am becoming because I feel like I am becoming more real."

Courtney recently ran for the mayor of Oakland. She did not win that race, but she is definitely handing the torch down in her modeling of what honest and ethical politicians are capable of doing . . . and being.

Sandy is dwelling in the possibilities of who she is becoming. "I don't know who I am becoming yet. I have an idea and I feel doubts every day if I can walk in those shoes and become it, but it is going to make me do things I have never done before to enact change.

"When I look at my three-year-old niece, or I look at some of these people that are in my world, I see the opportunities that can change their world as it has for yours and mine. I know I can be a part of that change, but that means I have to become a different person. I have been given a gift and a platform where I can do many things. I am still defining who I am going to be, but I get to work with an incredible team and people to help in defining what diversity and inclusion is while changing the way we work, live, play, and learn.

"You see these role models in life who have done these big great things. I am never going to be a Mother Teresa or a Gandhi, but there is a legacy that I want to leave. I am still finding my journey. And every day I wake up I am reenergized and reinvigorated. I see the blue skies and the greens in the trees and that's what makes me realize it is a journey at the end. I love it!"

> "Life is a gift, and it offers us the privilege, opportunity, and responsibility to give something back by becoming more."
>
> —TONY ROBBINS

Sandy is constantly present to what needs to happen next to keep her bigger game moving forward. She is enthusiastic and passionate about playing her game 100 percent.

Anne found that asking for help was a big change for her. After a short period of time, she no longer hesitated to ask people what she should do or what ideas they had. She knew people in the corporate world and in the foundation world. She soon found it easy, if she didn't know how to do something, to call someone and ask for help.

"I would do anything to make this work, which is what it takes to create a start-up. It is very important to have somebody at the beginning who will do anything to make it work, and for the Global Women's Fund, I was that person. I just kept thinking 'This idea makes sense. This could change the world.' My belief and my commitment and my clarity about this simple idea really being a world-changing possibility really appealed to people. People really wanted to find meaning in the world. People are looking for meaning in their lives. I know I am more empowered than I was. By empowered, I mean having a vision for change and feeling confident enough to take a step in the right direction to make it happen. Finding out you are capable of setting out a plan to move that change forward is very powerful."

> "Life is not a having and a getting, but a being and a becoming."
> —MYRNA LOY

Shari thanks her experience working with champions, where she learned for herself what it takes to become a champion in her own life. "I've been able to apply the core disciplines and principles of a fighter into all areas of my life—personal, professional, emotional, mental, and spiritual. I realize the amount of courage, dedication, and commitment it takes to be a champion. Champion fighters keep getting back up when knocked down in the octagon. They understand that winning doesn't come without blood, sweat, and tears. They are warriors that aren't afraid to stare fear and adversity right in the eye, and endure the pain needed to win.

"It has been a profound lesson for me, knowing and accepting that life doesn't come without punches and pain. I haven't become a champion because of my ability to avoid the knockouts. I've become a champion in my life because I keep getting up when I get knocked down, and refuse to give up, no matter how significant the setback. Being the manager of a fighter has been a true gift for me because of how it has changed my perspective on life and the way I overcome challenges. I now feel compelled to share this gift with others and empower them to uncover the champion inside them. I firmly believe it is within all of us, and I want to equip people with the tools they need to fight for the win, and rise victorious."

> "I think it's important to get your surroundings as well as yourself into a positive state—meaning surround yourself with positive people, not the kind who are negative and jealous of everything you do."
> —HEIDI KLUM

Shari is no longer afraid or apprehensive about reinventing herself, and there is definitely an increased confidence and a belief in her ability to conquer the things she sets out to do because of her experience.

> "There is not a beginning too small."
>
> —ANNE FIRTH MURRAY

Linda believes that "you create yourself through what you are committed to. You create yourself through the actions that flow from that commitment." She has designed herself to be dedicated to women's leadership around the world. She has learned how to be a very supportive and encouraging leader. She has grown the idea of the Global Women's Leadership Network from a small idea in her head, on a walk after work, to the international organization it has become, preparing women leaders to create major social change around the world.

She lives the GWLN vision of Whole Woman, Whole Leader, Whole World.

For me, I have become the kind of woman I never imagined I would be. I am confident, strong, compassionate, and for the most part, I am gutsy. Gutsy for the sake of my Bigger Games.

I ask myself the following questions when I am at a crossroad. You may find it useful to ask yourself:

Why me?

Why now?

Why bother?

Why not?

ASK YOURSELF . . .

- If you are playing a bigger game right now, who are you becoming because of it?

- If you want to play a bigger game, who must you become in order to take that first step?

- Complete this sentence: "I want people to remember me as the kind of person who . . ."

- Now go out and become the person you wrote about in the question immediately above.

Conclusion

....

MY VISION FOR YOU, GUTSY WOMAN

At the beginning of this book, in my tribute to Laura Whitworth, I wrote about her impact on me and on all the games I have played since she came into my life.

I've chosen to close *Gutsy Women Win* in part by quoting a deeply moving "declaration" from Laura's blog as a gift from her to me and now, from me to you.

> My declaration to you is that I will hold us to be generous with each other. That I will give by receiving and I receive by allowing you to give or touch. And you will receive by giving and by receiving from others. That we will choose who we will be in this arena, rather than get swept away by the challenges involved. And that we hold each other as big and brave. I can feel a twinge as I write this. How arrogant might this appear? I hope instead that it is perceived as an invitation for both of us to step beyond normal behavior, beyond business as usual. And to step into who we choose to be.

This triggers my final reflective question for you: "Who do you choose to be today and for all the days for the rest of your life?"

Oliver Wendell Holmes, Sr. said it so well: "Many people die with their music still in them. Why is this so? Too often it is because they are always getting ready to live. Before they know it, time runs out."

Don't let this happen to you. Stop getting ready to live and start living.

Design who you are becoming.

Be conscious about your design. Be intentional and purposeful.

As Laura challenges us, let's hold each other as big and brave.

I envision you will find that torch that George Bernard Shaw talks about when he wrote: "I rejoice in life for its own sake. Life is no 'brief candle' for me. It is a sort of splendid torch which I have got hold of for the moment, and I want to make it burn as brightly as possible before handing it on to future generations."

Embrace that torch and hold it for the moment to have it burn brightly.

It is your game to hand on to future generations.

I invite you to look deeper into your bigger game and to yourself as a game changer. You can find the support and inspiration you need to create your bigger game. Just ask. People are waiting for you.

Let's get gutsy and get going.

Together.

AN INVITATION TO
GET GUTSY AND GET GOING

I am inviting you to get into action. To Get Gutsy and Get Going.

Right here. Right now. No backing out.

I invite you to check out the website: www.GutsyWomenWin.com.

I invite you to sign up for the "Let's Get Gutsy and Get Going" Challenge that will walk you through The Bigger Game Model and apply it to your unique bigger game. Use the code "GWWBook" for a 50% discount.

I invite you to join us on Twitter @GutsyWomenWin

I invite you to join us on FaceBook:

www.facebook.com/GutsyWomenWin/

I invite you to connect with me on LinkedIn:

www.linkedin.com/in/patobuchowski

I invite you to join our email list to get inspirational daily quotes and the latest and greatest information from the Gutsy Women Win movement and to become a part of it:

gutsywomenwin.com/membership-site/join gutsy-movement/

I invite you to contact me with any comments, attagirls, input on what you need to Get Gutsy and Get Going, and any updates regarding your bigger games: Pat@GutsyWomenWin.com.

I invite you to invite me to come and speak to your groups and companies about How to Get Gutsy and Get Going and other leadership topics or to run a workshop on The Bigger Game. Here's a taste of me:

http://gutsywomenwin.com/mediapress/

ACKNOWLEDGMENTS

I saved this until the very last minute before publication, and, for me, this was the hardest part of the entire book to write.

I started by spending time thanking those who were directly involved in making this book physical and bringing it to the world, my editor and publisher. Then I continued by thanking all those who contributed directly to the book, the people in the book, as well as those who read and provided advanced praise and feedback.

Then I began to think of those in my life who support(ed) me and my growth in any way that led me to write this book, including my family, friends, teachers, clients, coaches, mentors . . . well, most everyone I ever learned from.

And then, I stopped.

I realized that acknowledgment, which is the act of expressing gratitude or appreciation for something, is one of my top values and is something that is best practiced in the moment.

Acknowledgement is a daily practice of mine. I hope that if you are reading this section and know me personally, you know how much I appreciate who you are in my life and how you have impacted me, and I hope that I tell you directly and often. If not, let me know and I will quickly remedy this.

So, from the depths of my heart, I sincerely and with deep gratitude acknowledge your contribution in making this book real.

You know who you are.

AUTHOR Q & A

Q: Completing your first book must feel satisfying. Can you discuss some of the joys and challenges?

A: This is the first book I have written solo. I was a contributing author to *Scrappy Women in Business: Living Proof that Bending the Rules Isn't Breaking the Law,* which is about the stories of eleven women whose career paths haven't always followed the yellow brick road, so I have a bit of writing under my belt.

When I was a little girl, one of my favorite places was the small library in my neighborhood on the northwest side of Chicago. I loved the quiet and I loved just being among all the knowledge and wisdom that were in those books. I sometimes think that I love words so much because my parents only had 8th and 6th grade educations, so we never had books in our house, although every day my dad read the *Chicago Sun-Times* from cover to cover and once a week did the same to *Time* magazine. My godfather gave me books for Christmas every year, and I adored him and his gift of words.

Words have always been very powerful to me. I majored in Journalism in junior college, but couldn't afford to go to Northwestern University to get my BA. Great writing can change my ideas about things, can make me more knowledgeable in the areas I'm ignorant in and also bring me to great imaginary worlds that help me escape the day to day.

They inspire me and move me to action, which is my hope for the individuals who read this book.

Q: Why this book, and why now?

A: I explain a lot about why this book why now in the book itself, but basically I work with The Bigger Game model developed by Laura

Whitworth and Rick Tamlyn. This model and its examples of how to put the model into use is the primary subject of the book. I have personally seen significant changes for the better in hundreds of people who learn about and implement this model in their lives. I wanted to be able to share the experience and help others see their lives from this perspective—to help them get into motion around creating their bigger games. I believe everyone wants to make a difference in the world, and this model can help them see where they are and where they need to go next if they get stuck.

Q: You interviewed many more women than those featured in the book. Do you have a couple of tidbits from the research files you'd like to share now?

A: I interviewed thirty-six women whom I considered including in the book. Some I knew personally, some were referred to me, and some I met briefly yet knew immediately that I wanted to get to know them better. I found that all the women I spoke to had a great desire to give back. All felt that although their lives were not always the easiest and there were great obstacles or major emotional upheavals to overcome, they wanted to give back to the world in some way. They were grateful for their lives and for what they had been given. There was a common element of feeling "blessed" to have come through what they did and come out on the other side a better human being with more empathy and compassion.

All these women were also very humble. In my opinion, they all began doing ordinary things in a very simple manner, one step at a time. Along the way, by staying in touch with "why" they were doing it, they found the "how" to do it and just did it. The book talks about why the "why" is so critical to our bigger games.

All these women were also courageous and found a lot of support in their family and/or friends who kept them going when they thought they couldn't go on.

I truly felt honored to be in conversation with each of them. It is really wonderful how your world opens up when instead of looking at relationships through the lens of "How can you be of service to me?" you ask yourself, "How can I be of service to you?" It changes our world.

Q: There are many other wonderful books on leadership, women's journeys, and self-reflection. What do you feel your book adds to the discussion—or, what makes yours different?

A: I offer a book about all three topics: Leadership, women's journeys, and self-reflection. What a deal! I also offer digging deep into a model that has worked for thousands of people. There is a Bigger Game movement that is happening and has been brought to thirteen countries to date. It is a simple model to understand. As Rick Tamlyn, one of the co-founders, says, "You can learn the concepts in just nine minutes, and it will serve you for the rest of your life." The model serves individuals as well as organizations. It offers a common language to use. It also helps individuals determine why they are stuck and then helps them consciously and with intention decide where they need to go next to get unstuck.

As one game changer says, "Stepping onto the Bigger Game board wakes you up—no kidding! The clarity, opportunities, hard truth, and soul-inspired passion that can be revealed offers you a choice—to be a player in creating a meaningful, wealthy life of purpose, or to live with the gnawing tension knowing that all of this is just one bold move away."

Q: In your work as an executive, leadership, and team coach you must see clients with all sorts of questions and challenges. What are the most common obstacles to success—beyond or perhaps including those you've described in this book? Do women seem to have different obstacles than those faced by men?

A: This is a very big question and books have been written about each of these elements. It has been my experience that women are faced with challenges in the areas of strength in presence when dealing with those in higher positions, which, let's face it, are still primarily men. I work with many women who are brilliant and technically astute but need more help along the lines of building their confidence, finding and using their voices, asking for what they want, speaking up with a diverse opinion, and, quite honestly, dealing with the opposite sex and the "good ol' boy" network—and out here in Silicon Valley that means the "Tech

Bros" who hold the majority of power inside the organizations. Yes, sexism still exists.

Q: What is one of the most surprising things you encountered as you researched this book? Likewise, what was something you expected to find, and actually did?

A: I think the most surprising thing is that the women I interviewed did not use The Bigger Game as a model for what they've accomplished, but in reviewing it with them, each and every one, even those not included in the book, were able to see how their lives and what they've accomplished and call "My Bigger Game" easily fit into the model.

What I expected to find was that all these women were driven by something that was greater than themselves. It was a "force" that drove them to do what they did and to cause them to continue even in very, very difficult times. Each started small—with an idea, or a yearning, or a calling they finally answered. They didn't know how to do what it was, but took one small step at a time, although it appears to anyone looking in from the outside that they took a really giant leap. They also became and are continuing to become the women they could only imagine they could be. That's what I loved about them. They are all gutsy women in their own right.

Q: Reading between the lines, a reader might sense a tone of urgency: Step up now and play your "bigger game," or you might never reach your full potential—or even find out what that potential is. Do you agree? At what point might it be too late—say fifty, sixty, seventy?

A: Never. It is never too late to start your bigger games. I think as we grow older we start to put restraints on what we are capable of doing. Then I begin to think about those amazing older women who are still living their lives fully.

On the cusp of her fiftieth birthday, Katie Couric became the first female solo anchor of a national evening news show.

At fifty-five, Ella T. Grasso was the first woman to become an American governor on her own, not as the wife of a previous incumbent.

At age sixty-four, Diana Nyad became the first person confirmed to swim from Cuba to Florida without the aid of a shark cage, swimming from Havana to Key West.

At seventy-two, Margaret Ringenberg flew around the world

At seventy-five, cancer survivor Barbara Hillary became one of the oldest people, and the first black woman, to reach the North Pole.

At eighty-five, Coco Chanel was the head of her own fashion design firm.

At ninety-five, Nola Ochs became the oldest person to receive a college diploma.

So, too old to play a bigger game? Ha!

Never.

Q: There's a lot of talk in the business world about the importance of "reinventing" ourselves. In today's fast-paced world of constant change, this may seem daunting. That "Comfort Zone" can look pretty comfy! Would you say playing a "bigger game" is an act of reinvention, or is it something different?

A: I had to reflect on this question for quite a while. I looked up "reinvent" on Dictionary.com and found three definitions:

1. to invent again or anew, especially without knowing that the invention already exists.

2. to remake or make over, as in a different form:

At sixty, he reinvented himself as a volunteer. We have an opportunity to reinvent government.

3. to bring back; revive.

So, reflecting on the question in this context I would say, yes! Playing a bigger game is an act of reinvention. It is inventing again or anew because sometimes we don't know our capabilities until we stretch ourselves to at least try something different. While "the inventions" (we) "already exist," we still need to continue to remind ourselves.

It is also a making over in a different form our life. We keep what is working for us, our strengths, those things that bring us joy and that we're passionate about and take those to a different form, to the form that we may have been afraid of before, but now can face because, after all, we are much happier, more productive, and have greater capacity for creativity when working with our strengths. Who wouldn't want to be all that?

And in playing a bigger game, we are absolutely working "to bring back; revive" who we are and who we are becoming. People come to me a lot because they have lost their passion in what they are doing. I simply ask them to reconnect to the games they played when they were children. What were the things they loved to do? What were the things that brought them happiness? What were they things that brought them laughter and joy? These are the things that bring us more happiness and fulfillment when we connect to them and bring them into our adult lives. These are the essence of bigger games.

Q: How often do you find yourself on a different piece of the game board? Does that change monthly, daily, hourly? How often should readers expect to find themselves on a different space?

A: We are always on the game board. That's what makes this model so useful. I am looking at this board and determining where I am and where I must go to next for the sake of my game. So it is always changing and flowing. I think that's one of the best parts of this model. You are always on the game board. You are always in the game.

Q: Is there anything you'd like to add that you didn't include in the book—perhaps to answer a question you often get from clients, friends, or readers?

A: There is something that comes to mind. When I speak to people about The Bigger Game model or run public workshops or work with teams, I always get the question "How can I play my bigger game if I have a job, a family, responsibilities that I have to take care of?" I believe that we are responsible first and foremost to take care of these basic things in our lives—shelter, food, families, etc. How I answer this question is that you must find a way to do at least one small thing every day to connect to your bigger game and keep it moving forward. Perhaps this is talking to one person about your idea. Writing down your thoughts or next steps about your bigger game. Connecting with your hunger or compelling purpose. Do things that may feel Gulp-y, even if they're unrelated to your game, just so you can get better at jumping into that feeling. Just do one thing, every day, to move your bigger game forward, and your bigger game will come closer to reality every day.

Q: You speak so highly and kindly about one of your mentors, Laura Whitworth. How wonderful that you were able to have that relationship! Do you currently serve as a mentor to others? What bits of advice or guidance do you offer that you didn't get from your own mentor— something you had to figure out on your own?

A: I believe that we all serve as mentors to others whenever we are able to share and learn from our experiences. My mom always told me that one of the challenging things about me was that no matter what anyone said, I always had to learn the hard way. I had to learn through my own experiences. She was right. I tend to do things the hard way, but I believe that is the only way that one can find out what works and what doesn't. What may work for you will not work for me and vice versa. We must find our own way in the world. We find out, through trial and error, what is our authentic self. Now, I am not saying this is easy, because it's not always easy; but it does help you stand more solid in who you are.

So, mentorship, yes. I mentor all the time when people talk to me and ask me for advice or coaching. I always share my experience, and I am clear that it is my experience and it worked for me, but in the end, it is your choice which direction you take. It is your gut that will tell you.

Q: What's next for Pat Obuchowski? Book? Conference? Sailboat? Garden?

A: I am a world traveler. I love new experiences and meeting new people of different cultures. I have trekked to base camp on Annapurna in Nepal, worked with the elephants in the jungles of Thailand, and rode dories in the Grand Canyon. I love to look outside my own life, which can become myopic at times. I want to continue to travel. My vision is to travel around the world and meet and speak to women leaders of other countries to help them find and play their bigger games.

Any invitations out there?

Q: Finally, if you could name the single most significant concept or piece of information you hope your readers will take away after reading Gutsy Women Win, what would it be and why?

A: Listen to your gut because you are the wisest person in your life. You know yourself the best and you know what makes you happy and brings you joy. My sister brand is called "Gutsy Women Win." This simply means that we, as women, need to get gutsier in our lives. Per dictionary.com this means: getting brave, courageous, plucky, bold, daring, fearless, adventurous, audacious, valiant, intrepid, heroic, lionhearted, undaunted, unflinching, unshrinking, unafraid, dauntless, indomitable, doughty, stouthearted, spirited, determined, resolute; informal: spunky, gutty, feisty, ballsy, skookum. (I love the meaning of this word—Google it!)

This doesn't mean that women who are not gutsy lose. Not at all. I am not comparing at all.

I simply mean if we get gutsy in our own lives—if we get brave, courageous, plucky, bold, and all those other words, we come out as winners in our own lives. We come out a better version of who we were before.

We are always designing our own lives, so why not design one that is the life we've always wanted to have . . . and maybe, even bigger?

I once saw a saying that I have hanging in my home: "When your life flashes before your eyes, make sure it's fun to watch."

That's what I'm creating.

So. Let's get gutsy and get going.

Together.

ABOUT THE AUTHOR

Pat blends her experience as a Fortune 500 Information Technology & Operations executive with her graduate education across Business and Neuroscience to help her clients achieve their leadership goals and go from good to great to gutsy. Her focus is on accelerated learning around change events, including on-boarding, promotion, transfer, growth, and mergers and acquisitions. Pat has fifteen years of experience in coaching leaders and teams in her own business, inVisionaria.

She is a contributing author of *Scrappy Women in Business: Living Proof that Bending the Rules Isn't Breaking the Law.*

Gutsy Women Win is her sister brand designed to help and support women leaders on an international level—because, quite frankly, we need more women leaders in our world.

You can contact this unorthodox optimist at: Pat@GutsyWomenWin.com.